Jack Corbett
MARINER

Jack Corbett
MARINER

࿓

BY A.S. HATCH

Afterword by Denny Hatch

THE QUANTUCK LANE PRESS

Denny Hatch can be reached at *www.jackcorbett.com.*

First Edition

The text and display of this book is composed in Garamond 3
Design and composition by Gina Webster
Printed and bound by The Maple-Vail Book Manufacturing Group

ISBN 0-9714548-2-5

The Quantuck Lane Press, New York

Distributed to the trade by
W. W. Norton & Company, Inc.
500 Fifth Avenue, New York, NY 10110
and by
W. W. Norton and Company Ltd.
Castle House, 75/76 Wells Street, London W1T 3QT

1 2 3 4 5 6 7 8 9 0

Contents ✌

Illustrations ~

To
JACK
Who was my rough but tender guardian and
mentor amid the hardships and perils
and in the unaccustomed duties
of my first voyage
At Sea:
who afterwards became a humble but useful
member of my household ashore
and the faithful playmate
and protector of my children
in their aquatic sports
and who died in my arms
this book
is affectionately dedicated

Foreword ✌

(From *The New York Times,* May 14, 1904)

DEATH OF A.S. HATCH
Once a Leading Financier —
Floated Great Popular Loan

Alfrederick Smith Hatch, at one time one of the most prominent financiers in the United States, died yesterday at his home in Tarrytown. He was born seventy-five years ago in Burlington, Vt., where his father, Dr. Horace Hatch, was a well-known physician. When he was a young man, he started a bank in Jersey City and a few years later formed a partnership with Harvey Fisk. It was while these two men were together that they achieved fame in the financial world. During the Civil War when the Government's borrowing power had been exhausted, the firm of which Fisk & Hatch were the partners undertook to float a popular loan of $500,000,000 in bonds. Although bankers in those days were not considered in the best of standing if they advertised, yet the firm sent broadcast over the country a circular appealing to the patriotism of the people.

The appeal to the country brought many curious replies. In one case a farmer traveled 800 miles to offer the savings of the family. He brought the money in a carpetbag and dumped it on the table in the office of the firm. It was a curious collection of coins and it took over an hour to sort them out, but when this work had been completed, it was found that the farmer had brought $17,000 in his old bag.

The firm of Fisk & Hatch was closely associated with Jay Cooke for many years. When the panic of 1873 came, the firm went under, but later resumed, after having paid all claims in full. In 1883, Mr. Hatch was elected President of the New York Stock Exchange and he was renominated and re-elected for a second term. A few years ago he sold his seat and retired from business.

Mr. Hatch married at an early age, his wife being Miss Theodosia Ruggles. The fiftieth anniversary of their wedding was celebrated only a few weeks ago. The widow, ten children, and many grandchildren survive.

Preface ✍

The incidents in this story are true. The characters are real. The dialogues are as literal as memory, after the lapse of years, will enable me to reproduce them. The personal experiences of the "Boy" are my own.

— THE AUTHOR

Jack Corbett
MARINER

PART FIRST
Aboard Ship

Chapter One ⌒

When I was twenty years old, but looking not over sixteen, I went to sea. I had been advised that sea air would relieve an asthmatic affection of the lungs that was giving me a good deal of trouble, and that if I took it rough it would be all the better.

So I shipped before the mast in a Liverpool packet, which was, in those days, about the roughest way, whaling excepted, in which a tenderly reared, half-invalid youth could take it.

It was in this way that "Our Jack" came into my life. (I do not call him "Jack" merely in the conventional way in which the name is commonly applied to sailors in general. He was really Jack by virtue of his christening, his full name being John Corbett.)

When I left my home under the shadow of the Green Mountains, I had never smelled salt water, nor seen a ship.

After I had been in New York a few days, at the old Clinton Hotel, then kept by one of the Lelands on Beekman Street where the Nassau Bank now stands, I realized that a first-class hotel was not an advantageous starting point for a seagoing career. It was not frequented by Jack ashore. And neither captains nor shipping agents nor boarding house runners were in the habit of searching among its guests for either able seamen or raw material.

Then I went to a sailor boarding house in Water Street. Here I fell in with a miscellaneous assortment of sailors of all nationalities—men who had sailed all seas and under all the flags that wave over them: and among them was Jack.

He was a typical old salt. Born in Ireland and brought up in a British man-of-war, he had since graduated a cosmopolitan—a mariner of any country under whose flag it pleased him for the time being to sail.

With his bronze-red cheeks, bushy whiskers, nautical attire and rolling gait, he could have walked out of the boarding house in Water Street and appeared on the stage as one of the crew of H.M.S. Pinafore, in the most natural way possible, without any artificial makeup whatever.

Jack took to me from the first day of my appearance at the boarding house, and in two or three days he had assumed a rough sort of guardianship over me which was amusing, but useful. He swore that I should go to sea with him, and that he would take care of me like a mother.

"Ye'll want somebody to look after ye, boy," he said. "Ye'll be no more use ter yerself aboard ship for the first few days 'an a suckin' baby."

As this was what I had begun to suspect, I was quite ready to believe him and to gladly accept him as my sea nurse.

I had abundant reason in the months that followed to be thankful for the good Providence that brought me into such a relation to this whole-hearted son of the Ocean on the threshold of my seagoing life.

With all his formidable appearance and gruff manner, there was a softness almost womanly about his mouth when he smiled. And a merry twinkle in his eye that told of a tender heart and a sunny nature under this rough exterior. And these were no false lights. They were the true colors, as I afterwards learned, of one of the most unselfish and guileless souls that I ever knew. He was by no means free from the external vices which characterized most of the sailors of his time. But they sat upon him so lightly, were so wholly external and so free from vulgar and offensive excess, and he indulged them with such a transparent absence of evil intent, and such almost infantile unconsciousness of wrongdoing, that the straightest-backed moralist, though he might have deplored the sins, could not have helped loving the sinner.

Jack's interest in me and his promises to take care of me amid the untried vicissitudes I was about to encounter, proved to be no fleeting fancy and no idle boast.

In this boarding house, which was a sort of big forecastle on land, I got steeped in sea talk. My own conversation began to be sprinkled with nautical expressions, and my clothes to exhale a faint odor of tar. I heard about voyages good and bad, ships lucky and unlucky, captains loved and hated. In the daytime, I wandered along South Street and the docks, sometimes in company with Jack, sometimes alone. I inspected the ships loading for foreign ports—coasters had no interest for me—noted their destinations, looked their officers over, and tried to guess what sort of men they were. At night I plied my messmates at the boarding house with questions about them.

One day a young fellow, the black sheep of a minister's family, whose acquaintance I had picked up at the hotel, and who had piloted me to this boarding house, came in and told me he had shipped in a four hundred-ton ship called the *Brewster* for a trading voyage to the Pacific. He had run away from home when a boy, and had made several voyages to different parts of the world. He was fairly well-educated, and a gentleman in his manners and speech, when sober and out of sight and hearing of the old sea toughs among whom he affected the broadest forecastle manners.

He wanted me to go with him. Under the glamour of his fascinating stories of life and adventure among the islands of the Pacific, I forgot for a moment my determination to make only short voyages for the sake of family and sweetheart at home and my fealty to Jack, and went with him to where the

Brewster was stowing the last of her cargo and stores, and getting ready for sea.

She had a full crew already shipped, and had no use for an extra hand—particularly a "white livered green one," the captain said, looking me over with undisguised contempt. I suppose my appearance was not inviting, viewed with an eye to robustness and muscle.

Despite my friend's pleading, he would not have me at any price, and I went dejectedly down the gangplank, feeling more insignificant than ever before in my life. This proved, however, to be one of the good Providences that attended my career as a sailor.

The next morning I went with Harry to see him off.

The *Brewster's* moorings were cast off, the tug alongside puffed and whistled, and the ship swung out into the East River. I had coaxed the captain of the tug to take me along as far as he was going, and bring me back with him. Outside the Narrows, the *Brewster* began to spread her canvas to the fresh northwest breeze. As the tug left her and turned up the bay, Harry swung his cap to me from the mizzen topsail yard where he was loosing the sail.

The *Brewster* sailed away, and was never heard of afterward.

When, thirty years after, I told Jack of my attempted treachery at that time, I thought he was going to cry, but he only said "T'were yer blessed luck kep' ye out o' that thar ship, an' yer bones from the bottom o' the sea."

A few days after the sailing of the *Brewster*, Jack took me aside and said, "Look here, boy, thar's the *New World*, a Liverpool packet, lyin' at the foot o' Maiden Lane, goin' ter sail tomorrer. I've signed articles for her at M_____'s Shipping Office. But they won't ship no boys at the office. I asked 'em. Ye'll 'ave ter ship as a boy along o' askin' the cap'n. Run right down to the ship an' ask for the cap'n. Walk up to 'im, bold like, an' tell 'im ye want ter go ter sea, an', ask 'im ter take ye.

She's an A-1 new ship, an' the cap'n's a good 'un—pious an' temp'rance, an' good natur'd as a pet lam' so I've heard 'em say as has sailed with 'im."

I started to go.

"Say, boy," Jack called after me, "if he says 'no' at first, don't ye give it up. Jest tell 'im yer old gent is a parson, an' ye've been kind o' wild an' most broke the old lady's heart, an' ye're hankerin' to be good now, an' goin' ter sea ter keep out o' the way o' temptation, an' ye can't think o' nothin' short o' goin' in a temp'rance ship with a good religious cap'n." And Jack chuckled at the thought of his own cunning.

I found the captain of the *New World* just coming up the wharf from the ship, a hale, well-dressed, gentlemanly man. He was one of the best of the old school of sailing packet captains, the recognized aristocrats of the ocean in the days when favorite packet ships still carried full lists of cabin passengers, before the steamers had crowded them out.

The memory of old-time, leisurely voyagers of fifty years ago still clings around those stately old ships, as that of land travelers of the same period lingers over the departed glory of the six-horse stagecoach—both since pushed from sea and land and forced to ignoble retirement by the relentless rush and power of steam.

I did not follow Jack's cunning program. Young and green as I then was, I had sufficient discernment to see at a glance that Captain Ebenezer Knight's piety and temperance principles did not make him a fool. Brisk, hearty, with a generous spirit and a keen intelligence shining out of kindly but penetrating eyes, a thorough sailor and a polished gentleman, he became my ideal of a commander.

"Are you the captain of this ship, Sir?"

"What is it, my boy?"

Before this brief dialogue was finished, I began to feel at home with him, and at the same time, knew instinctively that he was

not the man to try any of Jack's humbug and sentimental nonsense with. I told him the exact truth about myself in a straight-
forward way. I could not have done anything else if I had tried.
His shrewd eyes looked into mine, and just the suspicion of an
inquiring smile of genuine interest rippled the corners of his
mouth. There was no reason for telling anything else. I had
nothing to conceal or to be ashamed of. I was not an incorrigi-
ble young scamp running away from home. I was simply an
honest New England boy, son of a country doctor, with a gentlemanly training and a fair education, wanting to go to sea for
health and vigor. That was the simple story, and nothing could
have better answered my purpose with this open-hearted wise
gentleman of a sea captain.

He quizzed me by telling me how many young gentlemen of
my sort he had taken to sea with him who had fluked at the
first touch of hardship and had to be taken into the cabin and
nursed. This fired my pride and made me resolve on the spot
that I would drop in my tracks before he should ever have that
to say of me. I told him so, and added that I guessed the young
gentlemen referred to were not my sort. Then he went on and
told me, in an easy sort of half-confidential way, how he had
himself come from the Green Mountain State at about my age
and gone to sea under circumstances very similar to mine. He
told me how he had decided to follow it as a profession, and
how, by industry and pluck and attention to duty and persistence in steady habits, he had made his way through all the
intervening grades, from the forecastle to the quarterdeck and
the captain's cabin.

"Well, boy, you can go in the ship," he said, putting his hand
in a half-caressing way on my shoulder. "Go and tell the second
mate there," pointing to a cross-eyed man busy among a tangled
mass of rigging, stores, etc., strewing the deck forward, "and
come aboard tomorrow with plenty of warm clothes," adding

with a smile, "Don't forget that you are going to be a credit to our native state."

"Thank you, Sir. You shall never be ashamed of me," and I meant it. I think I would have walked up to the proverbial cannon's mouth without a tremor, just then, with that captain's eye on me.

I said to him, "Captain Knight, I have a gold watch worth, I suppose, a hundred dollars, a present from an uncle. I want you to take it, and if I break down it will pay for my passage."

"I don't think I shall need it for that purpose," he said, nodding encouragingly. "But it is not an article you will have much use for in the forecastle or that it would be prudent to have there. I will keep it for you in the ship's safe till we come back."

I went to the second mate. "Good afternoon, Sir," said I. He deliberately finished coiling a rope without looking up, and, when he had carefully laid the final coil and stowed the end, he raised his head. One eye looked straight at me, the other seemed to be taking observations along South Street, quite on its own hook. It was the peculiarity of that second mate's eyes, which I had many opportunities of observing during the voyage. They seemed to perform their functions altogether independently of each other. I have seen one of them watching the men on a yardarm furling a sail, while the other was apparently noting by the compass in the binnacle how the man at the wheel was getting along steering the course. I used to wonder whether they really saw two distinct objects in opposite directions at the same time, and concluded that it must be quite a convenient arrangement for a second mate.

"Well, what of it," he said in answer to my polite salutation. "And who the devil are you anyway?"

"I am going in the ship, Sir."

"A passenger, eh! Well, what business is that of mine?"

"No, Sir, before the mast."

"The devil you are. Who said so?" And the eye that had gone on duty concerning me when he first looked up began to take an inventory of me. The other was still busy somewhere up South Street. The eye took in my slim figure, my beardless face, my white hands, and my delicate and genteel appearance generally, which the rough and semi-nautical clothes that I affected at the sailor boarding house did not conceal.

"The captain. I have just made arrangements with him and he sent me to you."

"What does the cap'n suppose you will be good for in this ship? Oh! I see, he wants you to dance with the lady passengers on deck moonlight nights."

Instead of resenting the sarcasm, I laughed at the wit, which pleased him immensely. He softened. His on-deck eye winked at me, while his South Street eye remained as sedate as a schoolmaster's.

"Well you've come to me. Now go ashore, and come aboard with your togs tomorrow morning after you've kissed mama and the girls goodbye." As I turned away he added, "Hello, young feller, don't forget your dressing gown and slippers. They'll come handy when you want to join the cap'n in a cigar on the poop after dinner." He said this without betraying in his face, while I was looking at him, the slightest sign that he considered it a joke. As I reached the gangway and disappeared over the side, I heard something behind me that sounded like the gurgling of a brook. This mate and I became fast friends. He was not looked upon by the crew as of a genial temper, he did not have the reputation of being funny, for I never heard him mentioned as a joker. He was harsh and rough with the men when work was to be gotten out of them, but never to me. I used to think he was grateful to me for the pleasure he derived from our first interview. Years afterwards, when I had become a man of some influence, and his seagoing days were over, I helped him

to safe moorings in Sailors' Snug Harbor. He comes to see me
sometimes, and we talk over our experiences while shipmates
together For the most part his manner is grave and serious.
When I want to make him laugh I refer to that first interview.
It never fails to bring forth a chuckle, with an echo in it of the
sound I heard when I went over the ship side that day. Thus I
conclude that the joy of having at some time been funny is
perennial.

When I left the ship after my interviews with the captain and
the second mate, I went in search of Jack. I was certain that he
was hovering around somewhere in the vicinity. In fact, I had
quite a distinct impression that, while on the deck of the ship, I
had caught glimpses of him flitting back and forth between the
ship chandler's store at the head of the wharf and the saloon on
the next corner. Much to his chagrin I caught him coming out of
the latter, wiping his mouth on the sleeve of his jacket. He knew
that I did not approve of his intimacy with the saloons and he
had intended to so time his trips that I should find him inno-
cently inspecting the ship chandler's stock. Somehow he had
missed his reckoning, and crossed my course on the wrong tack.

"What luck, boy?" was his greeting, after some muttered
remark about "lookin' for an old shipmate round the corner."

"I am going in the *New World*, Jack, and am great friends with
the captain already. Come and help buy my outfit. You'll have
to tell me what to get."

Jack looked happy and was ready to enter at once on the
responsible and agreeable duty of guiding me in spending my
money.

That night Jack showed me a hitherto unexpected side to his
oddly assorted character. "Say, boy, would ye mind meetin' me
at Fulton Ferry a little after dark an' goin' wi' me to make a bit
of a visit? I may want ye ter lend me a hand."

Without asking him any questions or having the least notion

of what sort of a visit I was invited to take a part in or what I might be wanted to lend a hand at, I promptly assented and met him as appointed. I found him at the ferry entrance standing by the side of a large basket, like an oblong clothes basket of unusual size, with its contents carefully protected by a tarpaulin cover and with a stout stick like a small hand spike thrust through the handles at each end and protruding sufficiently to give one a good hold for each hand.

"Here's wot I want ye to lend me a hand wi'," said Jack. Lifting the basket between us we boarded the ferry boat. When we emerged from the ferry house on the Brooklyn side, Jack led the way down one of the narrow streets near the waterfront and then through an alley to a decent looking rear tenement house. Climbing the two flights of stairs to the third floor, we set down the basket on the landing while Jack knocked softly at the nearest door. It was opened by a comely looking woman apparently about forty years old, who recognized Jack with a cordial greeting.

She ushered us into a fair-sized room, the furniture of which indicated that it was living room, sleeping room and kitchen combined. Everything was of the plainest and cheapest sort, but scrupulously neat and clean. In a corner of the room was a bed in which lay a girl about fifteen, very white and thin with dark hair and eyes that formed a startling but not unpleasant contrast with the pallor of cheeks and brow. She stretched out an emaciated hand toward Jack and beckoning him to her, put up two thin white arms. Clasping them around his bronzed and hairy neck, she drew him down to her and kissed his rough cheeks.

Jack, the devil-may-care sailor, in the prime of sturdy manhood, whom I had heretofore seen and known only in the sailor boarding house and in the saloons and along the docks among his kind—a rollicking, reckless, horny-handed, hairy-chested product of wind and storm and sea and the rough and tumble of a sailor's life—and this frail girl, seemingly hovering on the border of the great beyond, whom a puff that would not turn a hair of Jack's whiskers might at any moment pick up like a fallen leaf and waft across—the contrast quite unnerved me for a moment.

Presently Jack disengaged himself from the clinging arms, and, standing in the middle of the room, introduced me with due formality as his shipmate. The girl looked at me with wondering eyes and a half smile crept over the woman's face as she offered me her hand.

I suppose I seemed in their eyes more fit to be the grocer's boy from around the corner than the shipmate of sturdy weather-beaten Jack. The contrast and incongruity could hardly have been less in their eyes than the thin white arms clasping his brawny neck had been in mine. Jack had apparently noticed their look of surprise and incredulity, for he added, "Yer see, Mar'm and Miss, wot I mean is he's goin' to be my shipmate tomorrer, for we're goin' to sail together in the *New World*. He hain't bin much of anybody's shipmate up to now seein' as he's never poked his nose outside o' Sandy Hook, an' I can't say as he's much of a sailor yet, but I'm goin' to make a sailor of him sure, and if he comes here wi' me after we gets back from this little 'scursion ter Liverpool ye won't know him."

This explanation seemed to satisfy them, and they looked as though they had no manner of doubt that Jack could make an Able Seaman out of a china doll as easy as turning his hand over if he set about it.

Then Jack removed the tarpaulin cover from the basket and disclosed its contents. First he took out a couple of dainty night robes, prettily frilled and embroidered, but of good strong, durable material; then some stockings of soft wool in a variety of colors; then a pretty wrapper of soft Japanese silk, picked up as he told me afterwards in Yokohama, on his last voyage; then some bits of ribbon, red, blue, and pink, tied in tasteful knots and bows for the neck. These, together with some books containing bright-colored pictures of ships and birds and fishes, and some toys and games, he laid on the bed beside the sick girl, who handled them one after the other with looks of unfeigned delight and little cries of pleasure. Then he handed a roll of some kind of soft, black stuff to the mother with trimmings and accessories for a dress. Then came packages of tea and coffee and sugar, and tumblers of jelly and jars of jam, and, lastly, oranges and lemons and grapes.

When all these had been laid out on the table, the woman, with an expression of strangely mingled pleasure and pain, exclaimed, "Oh, Mr. Corbett, how can we take all these things from you?"

"Now, look ahere, Mar'm," answered Jack in a grieved tone, "Considerin' as yer man, Ben Simmons, as was shipmate wi' me off an' on fer nine year, jumped overboard arter me in th' Indian Ocean, an' the ship agoin' ten knots, an' a tumblin' sea, an' saved my life, it's little enough I can do for them as belonged ter him. So don't yer go ter break my heart by refusin' any little trifles like them as it's a joy ter me ter bring ye an' the little gal." No feeling of delicacy or pride that might have made her shrink for a moment from accepting Jack's gifts could stand against these words and the look in his face and the tremor in his voice as he uttered them. Her look of hesitation vanished as she took both his hands in hers and thanked him with a full heart and moistening eyes.

Half an hour later Jack and I took our leave, after he had leaned over the bed, in response to a plaintive "Please come here dear Mr. Jack," and let her kiss his cheeks again.

We were no sooner outside when, bursting with curiosity, I asked Jack to tell me all about the woman and the sick girl and how he came to be playing Santa Claus in this fashion.

"Well ye see, boy, I had a shipmate as 'is name was Ben

Simmons, an' me an' 'im off an' on, cumin' an' goin', sailed pretty nigh all 'round the world t'gether. Five year ago when we was on the Coast of Africky in a Yankee brig loadin' elephant tusks, Ben 'e tuk the fever. Bein' pretty sartin 'e was goin' to slip 'is cable, 'e called me to 'im one day an' says 'Jack,' says 'e, 'I reckon this 'ere's my last v'yge, an' I'm goin' to lay my bones on this God-forsaken coast among the niggers an' wild beasts—an' I want ter tell yer some'at afore the delirium comes on an' I go clean off my 'ead.' Then 'e told me 'e had a missus an' a gal kid in Brooklyn 'an he gives me a paper with the street an' number on it, the same place we be just comin' from. An' 'e wanted me to promise as I'd hunt 'em up next time I fetched up in New York an' take 'em 'is chest an' see as they got the pay comin' t' 'im, an' to look after 'em a bit now an' agin whenever I was in hailin' distance of 'em. I give 'im the promise 'e wanted, 'earty shipmate fashion, an' my hand on it. 'E went wild next day an' was dead the day after that. An' I've kep' that promise, boy, right up to now, as ye seen wi' yer own eyes this blessed night."

I had been amazed, while seeing the basket unpacked, at the good taste and judgment displayed in the purchases, the appropriateness of the selections being out of keeping with the life and habits of a thoughtless sailor who had never had—as Jack had told me concerning himself—any home or female relations or domestic ties of any kind within his recollection.

I asked how it was that he was able to do a thing like that, and if he had any woman to advise and help him about it.

"Ye see, boy, I've bin larnin', an' it's took me nigh on to four year to larn that trick as ye seen it t'night. I made a bloomin' mess of it the first time. Why, boy, I tuk that little gal a new bonnet, all trimmed out with ribbons an' feathers an' posies an' things w'ich it was no more use to her 'n a pair o' wings, seein' as she hadn't bin out o'doors for five year. The little gal looked at it wi' eyes 's wide 's a pair o' ship's lanterns, an' then tarned t' th' wall an' cried in a kind o' soft sighin' way. The mother, she cried 's if 'er heart 'd break. I s'pose it was wi' thinkin' as her little gal 'd never have no more use for such fixin's. I felt as I'd like to go down through the floor into ten fathom o' water an' never come up agin. Then the mother she cheered up, an' that gi' me a notion of a way out of it. I asked 'er, if she didn't mind, ter put on 'er bonnet an' go wi' me a little ways if the little gal wouldn't mind bein' alone for a minute or two. Then I tuk 'er t' th' place whar I bought the bonnet and got 'er to trade it off for things as'd be some use to 'em.

"Another time I forgot agin, an' took the little gal a trundle hoop, an' a jump the rope, an' a pair o' skates, w'ich you'd 'low was nice things fer a little 'un as hadn't stood on 'er feet sence she war a baby. This time we didn't feel so bad, but we all laff'd a bit and then the mother an' me went out an' traded 'em all off agin.

"Another time I took, along o' the rest o' the things, a bottle o' whiskey, thinkin' it'd be good for the mother, ter perk 'er up a bit w'en she were down-'earted about the little gal gittin' no better. I'd forgot all about 'er tellin' me w'en we was a swappin' off the bonnet a year or two before an' I asked 'er to slip inter a saloon an' have a drink, as she was teetotal. W'en she seen th' bottle an' the label on it, she flushed up an' said, severe like, 'Mr. Corbett, I don't drink no such stuff as this.' I was knocked silly for a minit, but I righted m'self an' said, off-hand like, 'Bless yer 'eart, Missus, that ain't no drink, that's for bathin' the little gal w'en she gits tired wi' layin' in bed all the time.' Sence then, I hain't made no more such breaks, an' I've been larnin' right along. "

Then I asked Jack if it was true about Ben jumping overboard and saving his life.

"Bless yer 'eart, no, not a word o' truth in it. "

I supposed I looked a little shocked at this unblushing confession, for Jack hastened to add, "Ye see, it kind o' goes agin me to deceive 'er, but I got to do it. I 'ave to tell 'er them things to make 'er willin' to take wot I brings to 'er an' the little gal. She's kind o' high-strung, an' skittish 'bout bein' thought of in any way as a hobject o' charity, an' I has to steer a car'ful course to keep from runnin' athwart her feelin's. Ye seen t'night how she was shakin' in th' wind an' nigh' to gettin' a starn way on 'er about takin' the things, till I give her that yarn about Ben savin' my life.

"Last time I was there 'twere the same way, till I told 'er how when I were dead broke in Hong Kong, an' kicked out o' the boardin' 'ouse 'cause thar' was nothin' more to be got out o' me, Ben he stood for two weeks board for me, w'ich was a guinea a week, an' lent me a couple o' pound besides, an' I was only payin' 'er back wot were 'is.

"Another time w'en she acted shy about takin' the things I'd brought, I told her how as I was shipwrecked once in the Ar'tic Sea an' cast away all alone on a big iceberg, wi' nothin' onto me but a ragged shirt an' a pair o' trousers, an' I were picked up by a ship on which Ben were one o' the crew—we'd gone on separate ships that time—an' how Ben he tuk me to the fo'c'stle an' opened his big chest an' he says, 'Thar, Jack, take wot ye want. All as is mine's yern. An' then I told 'er I couldn't pay that debt in a hundred year, as it wan't the wuth o' the things ony, w'ich was considerable w'en I were nigh froze to death an' my own duds all gone ter Davy Jones, but the way 'twere done—just Ben fashion. W'en I give 'er that yarn she didn't yaw no more that trip."

"And were none of these stories true, Jack?" I asked.

"Lord no. All a pack o' lies from jib boom end to stair rail. Not but thar might ha' been true, every one of 'em fer the matter o' that s'fer's Ben's consarned, 'cause 'e were the bravest biggest hearted shipmate I ever know'd an' he'd a done any o' them things fer me if he'd ony had a chance. Ye see its all my fault an' not Ben's as they ain't true, seein' as I didn't fall over-board in the Indian Ocean, n'r go broke in Hong Kong, n'r get cast away on a berg. But them little sarcumstances wan't no way Ben's fault."

On the ferry boat, Jack fidgeted about and seemed quite uneasy. I was very thoughtful, for I had a good deal to think about between my experiences of the evening and what lay before me on the morrow. I suppose Jack must have thought from my sober face and my silence that I was sitting in judg-ment on what he had told me, for after a while he blurted out, "I say, boy, d'ye think them lies war so very bad"?

"Jack," I said, "I think they were the whitest, squarest, clean-est lies I ever heard of."

"Ye see, boy, I couldn't never stan' to see that little gal devourin' them things wi' her eyes, an' 'ave to take 'em away agin. I want ye to, boy, now we're be shipmates, ter un'erstan' as Jack Corbett ain't no kind of a common liar. In any or'nary business as consarned hi'self or w'en lyin'd bring harm to a ship-mate, a cat-o-nine-tails couldn't drag a lie out o' me. But I couldn't go agin that little gal, w'en a bit uv a yarn now an' then as couldn't never hurt a fly, an' might ha' bin true, 'd make it all right fer 'er, an' gi' 'er a clear sky an' a smooth sea."

The next morning, Jack took me to a slop shop in Cherry Street. After laying aside enough to settle my bill at the board-ing house, I had just $15.25. With this sum I must provide myself with the needed articles for a three months winter voy-age, as I had almost nothing fit to wear aboard ship.

My mother, who had a great dread of the water, and had dili-gently tried to impress me in my boyhood with the idea that one should never go near it until he could swim, had not been told when I left home that I was going to sea. She thought I was going south to teach, a common recourse in those days for young men and women who needed a change from the rigors of

It an' not Ben's as they ain't true, seein' as I didn't fall over-
[bo]ard in the Indian Ocean, n'r go broke in Hong Kong, n'r get
[ca]st away on a berg. But them little sarcumstances wan't no way
[Be]n's fault."

On the ferry boat, Jack fidgeted about and seemed quite
[un]easy. I was very thoughtful, for I had a good deal to think
[ab]out between my experiences of the evening and what lay
[be]fore me on the morrow. I suppose Jack must have thought
[fro]m my sober face and my silence that I was sitting in judg-
[m]ent on what he had told me, for after a while he blurted out,
["I] say, boy, d'ye think them lies war so very bad"?

"Jack," I said, "I think they were the whitest, squarest, clean-
[es]t lies I ever heard of."

"Ye see, boy, I couldn't never stan' to see that little gal
[de]vourin' them things wi' her eyes, an' 'ave to take 'em away
[ag]in. I want ye to, boy, now we're be shipmates, ter un'erstan'
Jack Corbett ain't no kind of a common liar. In any or'nary
[bu]siness as consarned hi'self or w'en lyin'd bring harm to a ship-
[m]ate, a cat-o-nine-tails couldn't drag a lie out o' me. But I
[co]uldn't go agin that little gal, w'en a bit uv a yarn now an' then
[as] couldn't never hurt a fly, an' might ha' bin true, 'd make it all
[ri]ght fer 'er, an' gi' 'er a clear sky an' a smooth sea."

The next morning, Jack took me to a slop shop in Cherry
[st]reet. After laying aside enough to settle my bill at the board-
[in]g house, I had just $15.25. With this sum I must provide
[m]yself with the needed articles for a three months winter voy-
[a]ge, as I had almost nothing fit to wear aboard ship.

My mother, who had a great dread of the water, and had dili-
[g]ently tried to impress me in my boyhood with the idea that
[o]ne should never go near it until he could swim, had not been
[t]old when I left home that I was going to sea. She thought I was
[g]oing south to teach, a common recourse in those days for
[y]oung men and women who needed a change from the rigors of

Simmons, an' me an' 'im off an' on, cumin' an' goin', sailed
pretty nigh all 'round the world t'gether. Five year ago when we
was on the Coast of Africky in a Yankee brig loadin' elephant
tusks, Ben 'e tuk the fever. Bein' pretty sartin 'e was goin' to slip
'is cable, 'e called me to 'im one day an' says 'Jack,' says 'e, 'I
reckon this 'ere's my last v'yge, an' I'm goin' to lay my bones on
this God-forsaken coast among the niggers an' wild beasts—an'
I want ter tell yer some'at afore the delirium comes on an' I go
clean off my 'ead.' Then 'e told me 'e had a missus an' a gal kid
in Brooklyn 'an he gives me a paper with the street an' number
on it, the same place we be just comin' from. An' 'e wanted me
to promise as I'd hunt 'em up next time I fetched up in New
York an' take 'em 'is chest an' see as they got the pay comin' t'
'im, an' to look after 'em a bit now an' agin whenever I was in
hailin' distance of 'em. I give 'im the promise 'e wanted, 'earty
shipmate fashion, an' my hand on it. 'E went wild next day an'
was dead the day after that. An' I've kep' that promise, boy,
right up to now, as ye seen wi' yer own eyes this blessed night."

I had been amazed, while seeing the basket unpacked, at the
good taste and judgment displayed in the purchases, the appropriateness of the selections being out of keeping with the life
and habits of a thoughtless sailor who had never had—as Jack
had told me concerning himself—any home or female relations
or domestic ties of any kind within his recollection.

I asked how it was that he was able to do a thing like that,
and if he had any woman to advise and help him about it.

"Ye see, boy, I've bin larnin', an' it's took me nigh on to four
year to larn that trick as ye seen it t'night. I made a bloomin'
mess of it the first time. Why, boy, I tuk that little gal a new
bonnet, all trimmed out with ribbons an' feathers an' posies an'
things w'ich it was no more use to her 'n a pair o' wings, seein'
as she hadn't bin out o'doors for five year. The little gal looked
at it wi' eyes 's wide 's a pair o' ship's lanterns, an' then tarned

t' th' wall an' cried in a kind o' soft sighin' way. The mother, she cried 's if 'er heart 'd break. I s'pose it was wi' thinkin' as her little gal 'd never have no more use for such fixin's. I felt as I'd like to go down through the floor into ten fathom o' water an' never come up agin. Then the mother she cheered up, an' that gi' me a notion of a way out of it. I asked 'er, if she didn't mind, ter put on 'er bonnet an' go wi' me a little ways if the little gal wouldn't mind bein' alone for a minute or two. Then I tuk 'er t' th' place whar I bought the bonnet and got 'er to trade it off for things as'd be some use to 'em.

"Another time I forgot agin, an' took the little gal a trundle hoop, an' a jump the rope, an' a pair o' skates, w'ich you'd 'low was nice things fer a little 'un as hadn't stood on 'er feet since she war a baby. This time we didn't feel so bad, but we all laff'd a bit and then the mother an' me went out an' traded 'em all off agin.

"Another time I took, along o' the rest o' the things, a bottle o' whiskey, thinkin' it'd be good for the mother, ter perk 'er up a bit w'en she were down-'earted about the little gal gittin' no better. I'd forgot all about 'er tellin' me w'en we was a swappin' off the bonnet a year or two before an' I asked 'er to slip inter a saloon an' have a drink, as she was teetotal. W'en she seen th' bottle an' the label on it, she flushed up an' said, severe like, 'Mr. Corbett, I don't drink no such stuff as this.' I was knocked silly for a minit, but I righted m'self an' said, off-hand like, 'Bless yer 'eart, Missus, that ain't no drink, that's for bathin' the little gal w'en she gits tired wi' layin' in bed all the time.' Sence then, I hain't made no more such breaks, an' I've been larnin' right along. "

Then I asked Jack if it was true about Ben jumping overboard and saving his life.

"Bless yer 'eart, no, not a word o' truth in it. "

I supposed I looked a little shocked at this unblushing confes-

sion, for Jack hastened to add, "Ye see, it kind o' go deceive 'er, but I got to do it. I 'ave to tell 'er them th 'er willin' to take wot I brings to 'er an' the little g o' high-strung, an' skittish 'bout bein' thought of in hobject o' charity, an' I has to steer a car'ful course runnin' athwart her feelin's. Ye seen t'night how sh in th' wind an' nigh' to gettin' a starn way on 'er ab things, till I give her that yarn about Ben savin' my

"Last time I was there 'twere the same way, till I when I were dead broke in Hong Kong, an' kick boardin' 'ouse 'cause thar' was nothin' more to be g Ben he stood for two weeks board for me, w'ich w week, an' lent me a couple o' pound besides, an payin' 'er back wot were 'is.

"Another time w'en she acted shy about takin' t brought, I told her how as I was shipwrecked once Sea an' cast away all alone on a big iceberg, wi' not but a ragged shirt an' a pair o' trousers, an' I were a ship on which Ben were one o' the crew—we'd g rate ships that time—an' how Ben he tuk me to th opened his big chest an' he says, 'Thar, Jack, take All as is mine's yern. An' then I told 'er I couldn't in a hundred year, as it wan't the wuth o' the thin was considerable w'en I were nigh froze to death duds all gone ter Davy Jones, but the way 'twer Ben fashion. W'en I give 'er that yarn she didn't that trip."

"And were none of these stories true, Jack?" I as "Lord no. All a pack o' lies from jib boom end Not but thar might ha' been true, every one of 'em ter o' that s'fer's Ben's consarned, 'cause 'e were biggest hearted shipmate I ever know'd an' he'd a them things for me if he'd ony had a chance. Ye s a New England winter but could not afford to go to more genial climes unless they could earn their way. She had consequently packed my trunk with tender and loving care with the things that a young gentleman going among strangers in the dignified capacity of a "professor" might be supposed to most need. There were plenty of white shirts carefully fitted and stitched with her own gentle hands; then socks and underwear adapted to a warm climate, etc. etc., and (the second mate was not far out of the way in his little joke) a handsome dressing gown and slippers, the combined handiwork of mother, sister and sweetheart, with scarcely an article suited to the tempestuous North Atlantic winter. This trunk, with the captain's permission, was eventually stored in the steerage passengers' baggage room.

My father had known all along that I intended to go to sea, and approved it, but in the kindness of his heart connived at the merciful deception and the blissful ignorance in which my mother provided and packed my outfit. We all believed that if she knew it beforehand she would be prostrated with fear and dread, but that if her knowledge of it should come with my first letter home announcing that I had really been on the ocean and arrived safely at some foreign part in improved health without having been drowned or devoured by sharks, her fear would be in great measure dispelled and she would gradually become reconciled. And so it proved.

After two hours of industrious shopping, consulting and figuring, we reached the following result, viz:

1 Corn Husk Mattress
1 do Pillow
1 pair Satinet Trousers
2 Blue Flannel Shirts
2 Thick Wool under do
2 Pairs Woolen Drawers

    2 Pairs Woolen Socks
    1 Oilskin Suit and Sou'wester
    1 Blue Dungaree Jumper
    1 Pair do overalls
    1 Monkey Jacket (second hand)
    1 plush cap (with ear flaps)
    1 Sheath Knife, with sheath and belt
    1 Tin pannikin
    1 Tin Coffee pot
    1 Iron spoon
    1 String of onions ("to keep off scurvy" Jack said)
    1 Canvass bag to tote them all in; and 75 cents left on hand.

Jack proved to be an accomplished bargain hunter among the stock of a sailor slop shop. He turned the contents of the shop upside down and dug into odd corners in search of choice bits that he suspected the wily proprietor had hidden away for the benefit of some favorite customer. He alternately coaxed and bullied and threatened to throw up the whole business so far as that shop was concerned and go to the establishment of a hated rival next door. He helped me to get, I have no doubt, fully twice as much for my money as I should have succeeded in getting if I had fallen into the hands of one of these sharks alone. Then we held a consultation as to what the remaining 75 cents should be invested in.

I was in favor of shoes, if any were to be had for the money, as I had only a pair of thin calf-skin boots, which I feared would prove quite unfit for service aboard ship. Jack said that we were never troubled with cold feet at sea. He assured me that as a matter of fact, many sailors went about decks and aloft barefooted from choice, even in winter voyages. He also considered heavy boots or shoes rather a nuisance than otherwise aboard ship. His advice was a jug of whiskey.

"Ye see, boy," he said, "yer sure to be bloomin' seasick at first, an' thar's nothin' like good whiskey for seasickness."

"Will it take a jug full of it to cure me?" I asked.

"It might, if ye had it bad; an' we oughtn't to take any risk o' runnin' short jest when ye might need it most."

Jack said this with a serious air, much like that of a doctor feeling the pulse of a patient whose symptoms suggest a bad case. He seemed to be pondering with a faraway look on the sad state of things aboard the *New World* far out to sea, with a very seasick boy, and no whiskey. He had priced and sampled the various brands the establishment offered and informed me that the 75 cents on hand would buy a half gallon of the favorite Blue Blazes brand, which was the right thing, and a jug to put it in.

Of course, the 75 cents went for the jug of whiskey.

I had such a horror of seasickness—the apprehension of which was not in the least mitigated by Jack's solemn manner and the grave motions of his head, sideways, and up and down—that I should probably have taken along a half gallon of bedbug poison if he had so advised. And there was not so much difference between the two after all.

This important business concluded, we stowed everything in the canvas bag, except the corn husk mattress and the jug. The mattress was carefully rolled around the jug in an ingenious manner contrived by Jack to conceal the latter from view.

"If the teetotaler of a skipper should happen to git his eye on it, overboard, 'twould go, sartin," said Jack.

I had trouble of conscience about thus deceiving my good friend the captain with whom my relations had commenced so truthfully and frankly the day before. But I recalled the threatened seasickness, and Jack's evident dread of the sad calamity of its overtaking me unprepared and without a supply of the gracious remedy which the united efforts of nature and the distillery had provided. I was for telling the captain about it and explaining to him that I had brought it aboard, not as a beverage, or as a means of unseemly carousing in the forecastle, but for medicinal purposes only. I thought it had been so many years, perhaps, since the captain had been seasick himself, that he might have forgotten, since he became a teetotaler, how necessary whiskey was to a seasick boy on his first voyage. I could have told him truthfully that not a spoonful had ever, up to that time, gone down my innocent young throat, and that I was firmly resolved that none ever should except in dire remedial necessity.

I expressed something of this to Jack.

"If you do any such fool thing as that, you'll be sorry when the sickness gits you, an' this blessed jug's at the bottom of the East River," was his comment. So I let him have his way, not without some humiliating suspicion that a process of moral deterioration was setting in quite early in my nautical career. We started for the ship, the bag over my shoulder, and the corn husk mattress and its precious contents lovingly folded in Jack's arms, the husks enveloping and protecting the juice, as in an earlier stage of their mutual existence.

When we reached the deck, Jack led the way through the indescribable litter that characterizes the deck of a ship on the eve of sailing: piles of rigging, fag ends of cargo, cabin passengers' baggage, steerage passengers' humbler belongings, chicken coops, pigpens, ship's stores, sailors' chests, and almost every conceivable thing that ever goes to sea in a ship, all mingled in inextricable chaos, waiting for the final clearing up while anchored in the stream or towing down the bay.

The *New World* had a double forecastle, level with the main deck and roofed over with a topgallant forecastle deck, the two compartments, port and starboard, having bunks for sixteen to eighteen men each.

The intervening space, amidships between them, was occupied by the great windlass for hoisting the anchors, and the bitts for making fast the tacks of the foresail. We made our way to the starboard forecastle where Jack selected the bunks we would occupy, one above the other, if we should chance to be assigned to the captain's watch and that side of the ship. He spread my mattress in the upper bunk, dumped my bag on top of it, and carefully stowed away and concealed the jug in a corner of the space under the lower one. Then he went ashore for his own kit, which made its appearance an hour later in a bright green sailor's chest on a handcart.

Jack did not come with his chest, and, after I helped the hand-cart man to place it in front of our bunks, I sat down on it and began to feel lonesome.

No others of the crew had appeared, which caused no little surprise, as the ship was advertised to sail at noon. I had expected to see them mustered on deck in wide-bottom trousers, blue shirts with broad collars, black silk handkerchiefs knotted loosely over their brawny chests and tarpaulin hats with long ribbons fluttering in the wind. True, I had noticed the absence of such rig among my companions of the boarding house—with the exception of Jack, who was always mostly dressed in man-of-war clothes. The crew wore an endless variety and mixture of dress, not at all of the traditional sailor sort as represented in pictures and on the stage.

The matter of nautical toilet, so far as the merchant service is concerned, was among the first of my disillusions. If my first introduction to sailors and sailor life had been on a man-of-war, it would have been different. I did not know then that it was customary for a Liverpool packet to be got away from the wharf by the aid of stevedores and longshoremen. And, when anchored in the stream, to receive her crew in small boats, at the hands of boarding house runners, the land sharks of those days, in all stages of sobriety, drunkenness, and insensibility, and with every variety of outfit, from the well-stuffed sea chest of the occasional thrifty sailor, to the miserable shoddy on his back and the nearly or quite empty bag of the improvident.

I did not know that crews of those handsome ships were made up in part of the scum of the sea, with a considerable mixture of the roughs and toughs of Cherry and Water Streets and with only a sprinkling of genuine deep-sea sailors of the better type. All this I found out later on.

After a while, I emptied out the contents of my canvas bag. I selected a blue flannel shirt, the satinet trousers and the plush cap, put them on and went out on deck. I wanted to be doing something or learning something.

The second mate was bustling about with his eyes busy fore and aft, each eye, as usual, apparently doing duty without the slightest regard to the other.

Another man fully six feet tall, with a big nose, big hands, big feet and a big voice, was shouting out orders right and left and lending a hand here and there in executing them. Presently another appeared and began to help the big man give orders, and to put life into things generally, while a fourth was stowing away bundles of new rope, cans of paint, oil, etc. in a large locker just forward of the cook's galley.

I approached the second mate and asked if there wasn't something I could do. One of his eyes recognized me and expressed mild surprise. I afterwards found out that sailors were not in the habit of hunting around the ship and appealing to the officers for something to do. They considered that they earned their wages if they did what they were ordered to do, when they were ordered, and left it to the officers to find out and notify them when their services were required.

The second mate evidently concluded that my greenness accounted for this unusual demonstration on my part, and the surprise died out of the eye. "Plenty to be done," he said, "but the Lord only knows what *you* can do aboard a ship. Go and ask Mr. Sargent there," pointing to the big man.

Mr. Sargent proved to be the third mate. The man who was helping him was Mr. Henry, the fourth mate, and he who was stowing away things in the locker was the boatswain. I presume he had a name of his own by which he had been called before he became "bo's'n," but if he had I never heard it mentioned.

I went over to the big man and repeated my question. He had not seen or noticed me before. He looked down at me from his six feet of height with an expression that said as plainly as words could have done, "What have we here?" But the look was indulgent. I was not a bad looking boy in those days, and my wide open brown eyes seldom failed to make friends for me of any well-disposed person who once got a good square look into them.

"A new boy I suppose," he said, his lips suggesting the answer to the question his expression had asked.

I found out before many days that this big third mate, with a voice like a fog horn and fists like sledgehammers, had a heart as big as the rest of him, but not nearly so tough. He took me to the side of the ship and showed me how to coil a rope and how to capsize the coil when it was to lie on the deck or hang it neatly on a belaying pin in the rail.

"There, boy," he said. "Do that to all the ropes leading aloft you find lying around loose."

I coiled industriously for the next half-hour. My work was not in the highest style, as I well knew by comparison with the more tidy coils that hung from the pins, but there was a lot of honest endeavor in it. My father had taught me that whatever was worth doing at all was worth doing well and illustrated it by the story of a man who had risen from a rather humble origin to a position of some importance in the community in which he lived. Being publicly taunted once by a man of higher degree but of less worthy achievement, with the fact that he had once been only a drummer boy, he replied, "Well, Sir, didn't I drum well?" to which his antagonist could find no answer, for the relative quality of what the two men had accomplished and the use they had made of their opportunities was well known to all their fellow citizens. This story may not be new to the rising generation, but it will not hurt any young fellow to have it recalled to his memory. I meant to live up to that motto aboard that ship; and I did to the best of my ability, whether it was in steering the ship or slushing a mast.

I was so absorbed in my work of coiling rope, that I did not notice anything unusual, until, I happened to look over the bulwarks in the hope of seeing Jack somewhere about. I suddenly became aware that the wharf and that the vessels moored on the opposite side of it, had all apparently gotten under way and were gradually sailing away from us in the direction of uptown. Then I found that we were cast adrift from the wharf, and a tug at the end of a heavy line astern was puffing and blowing and pulling at us with all its noisy might. In a few minutes we were moving clear of wharf and craft, out into the East River.

I was greatly worried about Jack. I thought we had started on our voyage and he was left behind. I was stung with remorse that I had not exhorted him more earnestly to avoid the saloons and to be sure to be on time. What should I do amid the untried vicissitudes and perils of the sea without Jack? And what would he do, poor Jack, drifting about among the still more perilous shoals and quicksands of Water and Cherry Streets and the Bowery without his green chest and me.

I had begun to realize very soon after our acquaintance commenced that the guardianship business was not going to be all on one side, that Jack needed me in some respects as much as I needed him in others. In all matters pertaining to the ocean and ships, to seamanship and nautical skill, to the comfort and care of one's self on board ship and to usefulness afloat, I was but a child learning my A.B.C. at Jack's knee. Jack was my oracle, to whom I looked up with as much awe and respect as I had ever felt toward the Greek professor in the Academy in which I had acquired the last of my education.

But in respect to worldly wisdom on land, to shore tactics, to prudence and thought, and to the care of one's self and one's belongings among the land sharks, and in the treacherous currents of the city streets, Jack was the baby and I was the mentor and guide. Jack was as conscious of this as I. Sometimes I would find him in one of the sailor dancehouses and I would pull him out of the arms of some painted siren who was patting his cheeks with one hand and going through his pockets with the other. Sometimes I beguiled him away from some gang of boarding house runners who were trying to get him drunk so that they could shanghai him, ship him off on some distant voyage for which sailors were just then scarce, and then secure his advance under the guise of a fraudulent board bill. When I berated him soundly for allowing himself to be in such dangerous company at all, he was meek and submissive as a lamb.

"Ye see, boy," he would say when I would offer some kind of apology for my interference. "Yer doin' jes' the right thing an' I'm blessed glad ye be lookin' after me this way—Jack-tar ashore, 's long 's he's got any money in his pocket 's a blunderin' fool all 'round the world, an' Jack Corbett ain't no shinin' 'ception. 'Twould be a marcy t' me if ye' could clap me in irons an' stow me away in the hold at the boardin' house, or put a collar 'round my neck an' lead me 'round with a chain painter, like a circus b'ar or a hand organ monkey 'gin I'm safe aboard ship 'n out o' sight o' land once more."

Jack had a considerable sum of money (the remaining proceeds of a long journey at high wages from which he had returned only a short time before I met him) cunningly sewed into various parts of his wardrobe. I succeeded, after much argument and persuasion, in inducing him to get it together and, after reserving sufficient for his reasonable wants during the remainder of his stay ashore, to go with me to the Seamen's Savings Bank in Wall Street and deposit the surplus. Subsequently, during our voyage together in the *New World*, he chuckled over this fund as if it were so much unearned money, picked up in the street. He, like the open-handed improvident class of sailors generally, was so accustomed to seeing all the proceeds of one voyage dissipated and blown to the four winds before sailing on another, that to have any money left over was like finding it.

Jack's mild dissipations and the widow and the sick were not the only drafts on his financial resources. No stranded, bankrupt, weather-beaten Jack-tar, old or young, ever appealed to him in vain for a drink or a meal or a lodging or a shirt, if Jack was satisfied that he was genuine. But gullible and easily imposed upon as he was by almost every other kind of fraud and humbug, he had a keen eye and an unutterable contempt for a bogus sailor with a whining story of having been "wrecked last v'y'ge, shipmate" or "wounded at Trafalgar."

I have seen him turn on such a one and, in a voice as savage as the snarl of a bulldog, shout, "Box the compass! Box the compass, ye lubber!" And if the man succeeded, as some sham sailors who had never seen the outside of Sandy Hook had learned to do as a part of their stock in trade, in stumbling through his lesson, Jack would shout, "Now box it back'ards! Box it back'ards, yer son of a land crab." When the man would go all to pieces at this, Jack would roar, "Get out o' this ye infarnal swab an' try yer lyin' jaw on them as don't know a honest lad in 'ard luck from a stuffed scar'crow or a wooden injun afore a 'baccy shop!" A few minutes later he would call out in a cheery voice to some forlorn looking mariner, "'Ere, matey, an' better luck ter yer next cruise," and toss him a dollar.

My reflections were interrupted by a great splash and rattle forward, a grinding noise, a succession of jerks, more shouting, then a sudden cessation of it all.

Then Brooklyn and New York seemed to be waltzing around and changing places, while Governor's Island, the ferryboats, the ships, and numberless small craft, joined in a general whirl. Our ship had come to anchor, and was swinging at her chain in a strong flood tide, in the middle of the East River.

Presently another tugboat came alongside, bringing the captain and a mild-looking gentleman whom I had not seen before. This was Mr. Hale Knight, the captain's nephew, and the chief mate of the ship. As I may not have any better opportunity to pay my tribute of respects to him, I will do it now.

He proved to be a model officer, though differing widely from the popular conception of a packet ship's first mate. His manner was as mild as his appearance. Like the captain, he was a gentleman, first, last and all the time. I never heard him swear, nor call a man out by his name, nor resort to violence of any kind, nor threaten any. He did not believe in the knock-down-and-drag-out style of discipline so commonly considered necessary in governing a ship's crew. I never heard him speak louder than was necessary to make himself heard. In ordinary times his orders were given in quiet tones. In the din and tumult of a tempest his voice could be heard all over the ship, but there was no harshness in its ring. Men who, on short acquaintance, assumed from his quiet ways and always neat attire, that he was anything of a milksop or a dude, soon found their mistake. He was a thorough sailor and brave as he was gentle. He was considerate of the welfare of the men, never overworked them when it could be helped, and personally saw that when they were sick they were properly cared for. It was curious to see how he won the respect and confidence and secured the ready obedience of our rough and motley crew by methods that were wholly at variance with commonly accepted theory and the customary practice in packet-ship discipline. To have seen him handle that ship in a gale would have taught a lesson worth learning to quarterdeck bullies of those old packet-ship days.

As I never believed it necessary to treat sailors as if they were brutes, or worse, I take pleasure in putting on record the fact that I never heard this man spoken of in the forecastle except in terms of respect, nor knew a man to sulk or skulk under his orders. I had reason to believe there was not a man in the ship who would not have been proud to do him a service, or to resent any disrespect to his authority. And we had about as tough a lot as ever gathered in a ship's forecastle. One old sailor expressed the prevailing sentiment when he said, "The man that won't do the fair thing by that there first mate ain't fit to feed to sharks. The mean cuss would turn their stomachs."

And now came the passengers in another tug. They were of three classes: first cabin, second cabin and steerage. The principal part of the ocean passenger business of those days was on the return passage; but on the outward bound passages there was generally a sprinkling of the above classes of voyagers. In the first cabin were a few tourists and invalids who at this season of the year (November) were seeking the balmy airs of Italy and the south of France. In the second cabin, some prosperous farmers, mechanics and tradesmen, who, having come over five or ten years before, and having found their promised Eldorado in the new country by acquiring farms or establishing successful business enterprises, were returning to see once more the old homes, to exhibit among their former neighbors, with pardonable pride, the evidences of their well-earned prosperity, and to bring out to the new homes parents, brothers, sisters, wives, children or sweethearts. In the steerage, less fortunate ones on like errands in a more humble way, or shiftless rolling stones, who had gathered no moss, or were disappointed and discouraged because they had failed to discover expected nuggets waiting in the streets and gutters to be picked up, were returning to such precarious livelihood as they could, in the old way among their former haunts. All these classes were represented among the hundred or more passengers who now gathered on the deck of the *New World.*

There was one who on account of his singular personality and his peculiar occupations aboard ship on the voyage over, became the object of special interest, and deserves a more personal notice. He was entered on the ship's first cabin passenger list as Professor Hendrik Van Speighel of Holland. It appeared that his mission to America had been for the purpose of discovering and classifying the different varieties of its insect population. He was a man to attract notice on sight, and his subsequent conduct fully justified the wondering attention that was bestowed upon him and his curious assortment of baggage as he came over the side.

He used to wander about the ship poking into all the odd corners wherever there were collections of dirt or debris of any kind with little instruments resembling miniature trowels, scoops, crowbars, etc., that he fished out of his ample pockets, and applying magnifying glasses to his eyes every now and then. Whenever he discovered any living thing, he deftly transferred it, with a little of the stuff among which he found it, to one of the curious little square receptacles with sliding glass covers of which he seemed to have an unlimited supply. He quickly became known among the sailors as the "bug hunter." Afterwards, with some vague linking of him with the objects of his pursuit, and floating memories of Bowery museum signs, the wit of the forecastle named him the "Human Bug." Indeed it did not require a very violent stretch of the imagination, aided by the association of ideas suggested by what seemed to be his sole occupation, to think of him as a sort of magnified and exaggerated bug. His short, slim legs ending in long narrow feet, his round and protruding paunch, his beak-like face with its green-goggle eyes, the peering pose of his bushy head mounted on top of a scrawny stretch of neck, and his high-collared blue swallow-tail coat with brass buttons, all aided this conceit.

The sailors looked upon him as a harmless old "Silly," and treated him with the kindness and consideration with which any sort of supposed mental lack seems to inspire rough and superstitious natures.

One day, while sitting on the deck mending torn sails, I became conscious of the presence of the Professor, and looking up, I found him regarding me with an enquiring gaze. The feeling came over me that he was studying me, as a newly discovered bug, without having quite decided yet where to place me in his catalogue. I imagined him setting out to classify me somewhat as follows:

Genus—Homo
Species—White—Americanica
Variety—Nauticus—Marine
Habitat—Oceanus Atlantica
Hair—Dark and Soft
Beard—A trace
Eyes—Brown
Note: Nautical appearance external and superficial only—exposed surfaces bronzed by wind and sun—where not exposed, skin white and soft. A curious specimen—must examine further.

Whether he made any further examination, or just how he finally classified me, I never knew. He was very secretive and zealous concerning his notes and the results of his researches. He was determined apparently that none of his treasures of discovery and information should leak out to the world until they should burst upon it in his reports to the learned societies that he represented. Fortunately for me, I was too big a specimen to be impaled on a pin in one of his glass-covered boxes.

Shortly after the arrival of the captain and first mate, small boats began to swarm about the ship, containing from one to half a dozen men each, beside the one at the oars, and as many sailors' chests, bags, or bundles. They were the crew. Those of them who were sober, or only moderately drunk, climbed briskly up the rope ladder hanging over the ship's side, or came hand over hand up lines thrown to them, clambered over the bulwarks, and dropped lightly to the deck. Among these, and, alas, not the soberest of them, was Jack.

Others, whose perceptions of where they were and what they were there for were hazy, and whose legs and arms were not to be relied upon, were helped on board by a series of boosts from below and pulls from above, mingled with a miscellaneous assortment of curses, exhortations to be "steady there," etc. Finally, all the small boats but one having discharged their cargoes and pulled for the shore, a fall was rigged through a block on the end of the main yard, with a sling on the end of it, and lowered to the remaining boat. The sling was fastened around something that looked like a rather large bundle of trousers, shirt, boots, and hat. Three or four men on deck caught hold of the rope, the bundle rose in the air, was hauled inboard, and dropped on the deck. Two or three others caught hold of it, dragged it forward, and deposited it in a bunk in the forecastle to sleep off the effects of its last debauch.

While this was taking place, I had looked on with eager interest. When I discovered, among the other things that went to make up the bundle, a human face with closed eyes and set features, my interest turned into the wondering awe that the young feel in the presence of the dead. I involuntarily removed my cap. I wondered if human corpses, in everyday clothes without coffins, formed a part of a Liverpool packet's usual cargo. I had heard the stevedores talking about "dead freight" and wondered if this was it. It turned out to be a lively corpse, however, when, about nine o'clock, it was tearing wildly about the deck, dodging imaginary sharks, devilfish and other monsters of the deep, until lassoed by the fourth mate with a dexterous toss of the noosed end of a rope that would have done credit to a cowboy.

At the turn of the tide, the big windlass forward was set in motion for heaving up the anchor, the capstan on the main deck was manned to take in the slack of the heavy chain cable, two tugboats, one on each side, made fast to the ship, and she headed down the bay.

All hands were mustered on deck for the ceremony of choosing the watches. The men took their places in line. All answered to their names except two—the man who had been hoisted aboard and one other who had succumbed soon after reaching deck. Both lay dead drunk in the forecastle.

We were thirty-six in all, thirty-two men and four boys. Those who were not able seamen were called "boys" without regard to age or size. According to custom, the crew was to be divided into two watches, called the starboard or captain's watch and the port or chief mate's watch. The men were chosen alternately by the first and second mates (the latter representing the captain's watch), and each picked out in turn the men he thought most desirable of those who were left.

When all the men in line had been chosen, the two who lay in the forecastle were assigned by the toss of a coin, neither of the officers having seen them. Then came the boys. There were three besides myself, all of whom were robust young fellows who had been to sea before. Naturally I was left to the last, and fell to the second mate. It was plain to be seen that he did not value me highly as an acquisition to the working force of his watch.

There was a friendly discussion over me, more amusing than complimentary to my prospective qualities as a sailor. The sec-

ond mate wanted to trade me off for one of the other boys, argu-
ing that as the first mate had, by virtue of his first choice,
secured the best man of the crew, it was no more than a fair deal
to give him another boy in place of the "green one." The first
mate failed to see it in that light. He ended the discussion by
saying that, as the captain had taken the young gentleman
without consulting him, the second mate might keep him in his
watch and make the most of him. As Jack had been chosen by
the second mate I was well pleased with this conclusion. I cared
more just then to be in the same watch with Jack than I did
about what they thought of me in the matter of muscle, in
respect to which I had no very high opinion of myself. I nursed,
however, a secret hope that they would change their minds
before the voyage was over, and had a grim determination to
give them cause. Before we reached Liverpool I was transferred
to the first mate's watch, and learned with pardonable pride that
it was at his request.

The following incident will illustrate the manner in which
sailors were sometimes sent to sea, and how little their own voli-
tion had to do with it. The next morning, the two men who had
been drunk in the forecastle appeared on deck. Looking about him,
one of them asked, "What ship 's this, an' where's she bound?"

"The *Pelican of the Sea*, bound for the North Pole," answered
one.

"The *Devil's Frying Pan*, bound for the Equator," said another.

"The *Sailor's Grave Yard*, bound for the west coast of Africa,"
put in a third.

"Shut up mates, tell the man the truth; how'd you like to be
fooled yourself if you'd been shanghaied," said another with
apparent indignation at the unfeeling levity of those who had
spoken.

"I say shipmate, you're in luck, you're aboard the *Flying
Demijohn*, loaded with New England rum in bulk in the hold,

and a cargo of gals 'tween decks, bound for Californy to load back with gold. Everybody is to have all the rum he can hold goin' out, and as much of the home cargo as he can walk off with, when we're discharged."

"Look here, matey, I've got a patent jaw greaser in my chest for a prize for the boss liar of the fo'c'sle of this 'ere ship, whatever her name may be, or wheresomever she be bound to. It's yours, matey, to command," said the man. Then he walked deliberately away, climbed the ladder to the topgallant forecastle, went forward and looked over the bow. The *New World* had for a figurehead a wooden statue of Columbus, leaning forward at an angle of forty-five degrees and holding out the globe in his right hand. The man leaned forward over the cathead until he caught sight of the figure, with which he apparently carried on a conversation, wagging his head and gesticulating with his fists. When he came back to the group of sailors with whom he had held the dialogue above related, he quietly said, "It's all right. Christopher an' I have been shipmates afore, an' I'd as lief he'd pilot me across this 'ere frog pond as any other woodenheaded old admiral that ever sailed."

Then he turned to with the rest, and nothing more was said on the subject, except that one man remarked in a soliloquizing way, "There's nothing like Cherry Street rum with a little opium juice in it, to send a man aboard ship so that he don't know Christopher Columbus from the Pope o' Rome 'til next day, besides savin' him the trouble of climbing the side ladder by giving him a h'ist in the slings."

When I had reached this point in my narrative, and was reading over what I had written to my assembled family one evening, my youngest daughter (aged 18) broke in with, "It seems to me you are a long time getting to sea, Papa. You have written enough to make a book already and you haven't got out of the bay yet."

"My dear," I said, "you have no idea of what it is to get a young fellow off to sea on his first voyage. You've never tried it."

"Well, Papa," she persisted, "if your ship is as slow as your story and you really cross the ocean it will be ages before you get back."

"Well, then my dear, suppose I leave out all about the Brooklyn Bridge and the Statue of Liberty and —"

"Oh, papa, you goose, they weren't there then."

"Right, my dear. Well, suppose I leave out whatever was there, and get outside of Sandy Hook at once."

"I think you had better," she said.

Chapter Two ~

Having dropped tugboats and pilot, with all plain sail set and straining at the yards in a strong northwest wind, the *New World* was laying her course for the Gulf Stream.

There was a buoyancy in her rise and fall to the ocean swell, and a sort of exultant dash in the way she threw the spray from her bow that seemed to say she was glad to be free at last of the wharf, the anchor, and puffing steam tugs, clear of shoals and buoys and muddy channels, with the broad ocean before her and fathomless depths of blue and briny water under her keel. The ocean too seemed glad to welcome her, and tossed her on its bosom and caressed her sides and smiled in the bright sunlight as if in playful satisfaction, while the rush and whistle of the wind through the rigging was not without its note of gladness.

All this seeming exhilaration of ship and sea and wind was contagious. Passengers and crew caught it and reveled in it, forgetful for the time of the coming perils of storm and fog, and of the horrors of impending seasickness.

Towards night I was on the poop aft, where I had been sent for some trifling task. When it was finished, I lingered for a last look at the land now fast sinking from sight astern. My blood had been racing and my nerves thrilling all day with the general exhilaration that had pervaded the ship, and with the excitement of the novelty of it all to me. Mingling with these feelings there now came a pensive mood, softening but not subduing them. As the twilight gathered, I realized for the first time that I was losing sight of the land on which all my life had been spent. The sun went down in a blaze of glory behind the Highlands. Fleecy clouds, through which gleamed streaks and patches of blue sky, hung from the zenith down the western sky, forming themselves into strange and fantastic shapes, and taking on brilliant hues of crimson and gold and purple and orange as they neared the horizon.

Then, as the deepening twilight lost itself in darkness, the twin flashes of the Highland Lights shot out over the sea. The outline of the coast, which had grown dim and hazy, disappeared, and the two lights were all that remained in sight of my native land. I had never seen them before and did not know what they were. But as the last visible links between my heart— now filled with tender memories—and what I had left behind, the Lights came to represent to me home, kindred, friends, country, and all that I loved. As I looked at them, they became to my quickened imagination a pair of watchful eyes, taking note of all the ships that went out to sea and the human lives and interests that went with them.

Then my mother's soul seemed to come into the eyes, now grown soft and tender, as if following, with anxious yearning gaze, the boy whom she was lovingly and prayerfully committing to the ocean and to God. Afterwards, on the return voyage, I used to think of them, especially in the dark nights, as watching there still, with unfailing constancy, to guide and welcome us home.

The next day was much the same—all blue sky and bright sunshine and smiling ocean and bounding ship—but to many of the passengers who had been so lively and gay the day before, it was very much *not* the same. The dire malady of the sea had begun to get in its work. Many of them had reached the condition in which it was a matter of utter indifference to them whether the sky was blue or green, whether the ship was going ahead or astern or sideways, whether the wind was north, south, east, or west, or up and down. If only, they thought, this horrid motion could be stopped that was turning their internal arrangements upside down and mixing up their stomachs and their heads until they were uncertain which it was that was making the other so deathly sick. But the persistence of the sea in making mountains and valleys of itself, and that of the ship in climbing up the one and plunging into the other, were piti-less, and, to their sick imaginations, seemed eternal.

So far I had escaped. I suppose the bracing air and the forget-ting of myself in the effort to understand the orders that were given and to have a hand in executing them, had enabled me to resist longer than the more indolent and unoccupied passengers. I had, even in the watches below, in my first experience of sleep-ing in a ship's forecastle, withstood the mingled odors of grease, tar, bilge water, lamp smoke, tobacco smoke and whiskey-laden breaths, which pervaded that place of repose; and, though my corn husk mattress and pillow seemed more suggestive of cobs than husks, I had slept the sleep of a tired boy. But my turn was to come.

Toward night the sky became overcast. The crests of the waves no longer glistened in the rays of unclouded sunlight. The swells lost their playful air and looked sullen and threatening. A dull grey became the prevailing hue. The merry note in the whistling of the wind was no longer distinguishable, and all the sounds given out from spars and sail and rigging were in a minor key. The ship herself seemed to grow serious and to be bracing her-self for earnest work. The lapping of the water along her sides had lost its caressing murmur and become a succession of vicious slaps. The officers of the watch on deck went below one after the other and reappeared in their rubber coats. The old sailors looked at sky and sea, peered along the horizon, shook their heads and told each other it was "goin' to be a nasty night."

By the next morning I did not need any explanation of what kind of a night that was. We had the first watch (8 to 12 o'clock p.m.) below decks that night; the chief mate's watch was on deck. We finished supper, smoked our pipes, and turned in. I had just dropped off to sleep and was groping in a confused dream in which things afloat and ashore were perplexingly mixed up, when there broke into my dream a tremendous pounding which at first seemed to be on the top of my head, but proved to be on the forecastle deck right over my bunk, accompanied by the cry "Starbolins Ahoy! All hands on deck!" Then before I was sufficiently wide awake to know what it was all about, I felt a vigorous shake and distinguished Jack's voice saying "Turn out, boy, and don't ye be behind the rest." Then the cry was repeated with a noisy accompaniment made up of the tramping of feet, the sound of coils of rope thrown to the deck, the rattling of blocks, the wild flapping of canvas, the roaring of the wind, the swash and splash of huge volumes of water, and loud shouts of the officers with answering "Aye, aye, Sirs" from the men. I realized that we were in a gale, and all hands had been called to shorten sail.

I sprang out of my bunk, landed on Jack's shoulders, and from there, with a violent lurch of the ship, rolled in an ignominious bundle under the bunks on the lee side of the forecastle. I scrambled out, and, after several efforts, and some more rolling and scrambling, succeeded in getting to my feet with a tight grip on the leg of a sailor who was just turning out above me, until, with the weather roll of the ship and a vigorous kick of the sailor's leg, I landed on top of Jack's chest with one elbow in his stomach and the other on the edge of his bunk, and my heels in the air. As I had turned in with my clothes on, the making of my toilet for the deck was not an elaborate affair—in fact it consisted in finding my cap, and then finding my head to put it on. I had perceived such strong indications that the saltwater was either shrinking my light calfskin boots, or swelling my feet, that I was afraid to pull off the boots when I turned in, for fear I might not be able to get them on again.

I was ready to go on deck about as soon as any of them, but whether I should get there feet first or head first or all in a heap, seemed very uncertain. The motion of the ship was very different from anything I had experienced before. The easy rise and fall to the long ocean swells that I had thought so graceful and exhilarating, had given place to a succession of violent and contradictory motions, that, to a landsman, baffled all calculations as to what would come next, and that it is impossible to describe.

One minute she seemed to be preparing to stand up straight on her stern, then to squat on her haunches, and in another moment, with stern high in the air, to be heading for the bottom of the sea. These up and down motions, fore and aft, were varied with sudden interruptions in which for a few seconds she seemed to stand still and tremble all over. The motions, and her sickening rolls to port and starboard, made me feel as if everything, my stomach included, was going to roll overboard.

The scene on deck was to a novice one of utter and inextricable confusion. The night was dark. Occasional flashes of vivid lightning revealed for a second the tumbling sea, the swaying rigging, the tattered fragments of torn sails, with startling distinctness, only to have them all swallowed up in a darkness more intense and impenetrable.

Groups of sailors were tugging at ropes here and there; others were making their way aloft and creeping out on the swaying yards. Officers were going about the deck flashing their lanterns and shouting orders in voices hoarse with the effort to rise above the din and roar of gale and sea and creaking ship. The crests of the waves, as they came tumbling toward the ship, gleamed with phosphorescence, and as they swept away to leeward, rising high in the air while the ship slid down their glistening sides, they looked like rolling hills of silvery fire.

Every little while, in some peculiar pause or motion of the ship, the trained senses of the old sailors would catch a familiar warning, and the cry, "Stand by there; hold hard" would give it voice. Then, with a blow like a thousand sledgehammers, a breaking wave would strike her and a torrent of water would come pouring over the bulwarks.

The deck was wet and slippery, and, to my unaccustomed feet, worse than nothing as a place to stand on. I might as well have tried to walk the waves themselves. One minute it would be a slippery precipice down which I was sliding, and the next, a watery hill up which I was vainly trying to climb—both these exercises being performed for the most part on my hands and knees. Now the deck would seem to be coming up to slap me in the face, and then to be dropping away from under me.

Each sea that came aboard found in me a helpless victim to be tumbled without ceremony into the lee scuppers with mouth and eyes full of salt water. Finally, in a brief lull, I succeeded in climbing up to windward and getting hold of a belaying pin in the weather rail. As the bulwarks were higher than my head, I was comparatively secure so long as I could hold on. Presently something ran up against me and a bull's-eye lantern flashed in my face. It was the second mate. "What are you doing here?"

"Holding on, sir."

"Well, you had better go and hold on to the end of the main topsail halyards there," turning his bull's-eye to where a line of men were hauling and singing as they hauled.

I set out to do as I was bid, and partly sliding on my feet and partly crawling on my hands and knees, I reached the rope, and, catching hold of it behind the last man, got to my feet, and, when the word in the song which is the signal to haul next came round, I hauled with the rest. I did so well that time that I was quite elated. Though I was very unsteady on my feet and beginning to feel uneasy about my stomach and dizzy in my head, I even joined in the chorus next time. Just as the moment to haul came again, a tremendous lurch of the ship to leeward took me off my feet. I instinctively clung to the rope as I went down into the lee scuppers, which I had visited so many times before that night. Half the men went with me. When I heard the torrent of curses that followed, and the indignant enquiries as to "Who in h___ did that," I was glad it was so dark.

A few minutes later I found it convenient to climb up on top of the spare spars that were ranged along that side of the ship, and, hugging a back stay with one arm and steadying myself on the rail with the other, to hang my head over the side and pay my first tribute to Neptune. Then I slid down to the deck and tried again to make myself useful. I got hold of the first rope I could feel my way to where men were pulling. But there was no pull in me. I was thoroughly seasick. I visited the side of the ship two or three times more, and then suddenly thought of the jug of whiskey.

Blessing Jack for his thoughtfulness in providing for this emergency, I made my way to the forecastle, and, reaching under Jack's bunk, felt for the jug. I found it at last, and drew it out from its hiding place. I uncorked it, and putting my lips to its mouth began to tip it up very gently. I did not want to get too much at once. The pitching and rolling of the ship, which was much more emphatic in the forecastle than on deck amidships, made it rather difficult to handle the jug as carefully as I wished. I felt no whiskey wetting my lips, and I tipped the jug a little more; still no whiskey. I continued gradually tipping it a little at a time and inclining my head backward as I tipped, until my nose was pointing to the deck above and the jug was straight on end. *Not a drop.*

Then I took the jug from my mouth, and put it to my nose,

thinking I had made a mistake and got hold of the wrong jug. There was no mistaking the smell. It carried me back to the slop shop in Cherry Street, where at Jack's invitation I had inhaled it to gratify his desire that I should recognize the excellence of his choice. I was puzzled. I tried the cork to see if it fitted tight. I concluded it did and that the whiskey could not have leaked away.

Then I began to remember some things that I had not particularly noticed at the time. I remembered that Jack had seemed to have frequent errands to the forecastle the day before. Once it was to sharpen his sheath knife which had suddenly become dull. Then it was to get a palm that fitted his hand better than the one he was using in mending a sail. Another time it was to get a new sail needle to replace one he had just broken, and so on.

I also recalled that several times while lying in my bunk half awake and half asleep the night before, I had heard Jack moving about, and wondered why he was so restless and wished he would get quiet and go to sleep. I had heard at such times an occasional gurgle which I attributed to bilge water under the forecastle floor.

I had also heard Jack heave a long-drawn sigh once in a while, and wondered what was troubling the poor fellow's soul. Once or twice there had been a sound as of sucking and smacking of the lips such as old sailors sometimes give out when their pipes draw hard, and I had concluded that Jack was soothing his troubles, whatever they were, with a smoke. An odor of whiskey had floated around me, but as this was one of the normal conditions of the atmosphere of the forecastle the first two or three days of the voyage, I had not given it any thought. But now all these things, each so insignificant in itself, grouped themselves together and forced upon my mind a reluctant suspicion that the contents of the jug had gone down Jack's throat. The disloyalty to Jack which this suspicion implied troubled me. But I could not dismiss it, and Jack's conduct next day confirmed it.

"I was seasick last night, Jack," I said.

Jack's eyes were gazing to windward with a faraway look in them.

"I took a pull at the whiskey jug," I continued.

"Didn't it do you good?" he said, and I thought there was the suspicion of a suppressed twinkle in his eye.

"I think it would have done me lots of good if I could have got anything out of it, but somehow the whiskey wouldn't run and I couldn't swallow the jug. Do you think it was cold enough to freeze it, Jack?"

"Look there boy! Did ye ever see a school o' porpoises? There's a thousand of 'em if there's one." I knew then where the sovereign remedy that was to heal my seasick woes had gone. But Jack never squarely owned up to it, until thirty years after, as will be related in the second part of this narrative.

After giving up the effort to extract whiskey from the jug, and feeling very sick and dizzy, I curled myself up on top of Jack's sea chest and, holding on by the edge of his bunk, gave myself up to a contemplation of my forlorn condition, though too proud to yield to it to the extent of crawling into my bunk and owning myself knocked out. I was soaking wet, having been drenched by every sea that had broken over the ship. I was bruised and sore with the knocking about to which I had been subjected almost without intermission for nearly three hours. It seemed as though every individual bone and muscle in my body was aching. My hands were blistered with hauling on the wet ropes and sprawling on the deck. My clothes were torn, my cap was gone, whether overboard, or kicking about the deck somewhere, I did not know—or care—just then.

The big third mate came into the forecastle looking for skulkers. His bull's-eye lighted on the sorry bundle of wet clothes and sick boy crouching on Jack's sea chest.

"Who is this skulking here? Come now get out on deck there quick."

"Yes, Sir, I was just going," and I raised myself up and tried to get my feet under me.

As he came nearer and recognized the "new boy" his voice softened.

"Never mind, stay where you are. It's the best place for you, and I guess we'll be able to work the ship through this flurry without you. Tumble into your bunk and have it out till morning."

My pride relieved by the thought that I was obeying orders, I climbed in, braced my back against the bulkhead and my knees against the front board, and went to sleep, steaming in my wet clothes like a hot boiled potato.

It is only fair that I should record here to my own credit that this was the last and only time I was incapacitated for duty or that I ever sought the seclusion of the forecastle when my watch was on deck.

The next day was clear and bright. All traces of the night of storm and confusion had passed, except that a heavy sea was rolling into which the ship, braced sharp on the wind, was roughly pitching. We were called for the forenoon watch at eight o'clock, and, after a breakfast of hard tack and hot coffee which I thoroughly relished, I was ready to go on deck with the rest. I had experienced my first and last seasickness, and, except that I was a little stiff and sore with the bruises I had received, was as good as new. The fresh northeast wind that came over the weather bow, filling every stitch of canvas and stretching the sails like drumheads, was invigorating. It was a good day for a landsman to practice getting his sea legs, and I made the most of it.

Before night came I had made good progress in mastering the art of walking a pitching and tumbling deck, and, with an occasional wild grip at a belaying pin or whatever other fixed object came in my way, I managed to keep my feet for the most part.

The next two or three days were uneventful. We had strong rough seas, but the weather was fine and bracing. Jack was particularly attentive and devoted to me, as if to make amends for his sad lapse in the matter of the whiskey, his solicitude for my welfare and his humble way of showing it being, all unconsciously to himself, a silent confession of his guilt, more eloquent than words.

He mended my torn clothes, patched my boots, washed my flannel shirts (except when I let the sea do it by towing them overboard at the end of a line) and made me a pair of duck trousers out of the remnants of a torn sail. He taught me how to knot and splice and how to box the compass. He gave me much valuable instruction and advice about going aloft, tying reef points, passing gaskets, steering the ship, against the time when I should be expected to perform these duties. For these first few days my nautical accomplishments did not go beyond swabbing the decks, coiling ropes, polishing the brass top of the main deck capstan, looking after the pigs and chickens, and tarring strips of canvas for parceling the rigging,

My first experience with the tar bucket was in this wise.

The boatswain called me to him the first day out and took me to where there was a pile of canvas strips a couple of inches wide lying on the deck and a bucket of tar standing beside them. "There youngster," he said, "you just turn to and cover them strips of canvas with tar, and roll 'em up like this," and he showed me how to roll them up like a surgeon's bandage.

I looked about me for some kind of implement adapted to the purpose, and seeing none, I asked him: "What shall I put the tar on with, Sir?" With a laugh he said: "Put it on with this," and seizing hold of my right arm, he jammed my hand into the tar bucket up to the wrist, and then pulling it out and holding it up to view, dripping with the black and sticky stuff, remarked,

"There, I don't believe your ma would know that lily white flipper now if she should see it," and walked away.

I took the hint, and went to work tarring the strips of canvas with nature's implement, which was the very best for the purpose that could be contrived. When I had finished, I set to work to clean the surplus tar from my hands by scraping with my sheath knife. One of the boys seeing my dilemma said: "Come along with me, and I will show you a better way than that."

He led me to a barrel standing by the door of the cook's galley in which all the different kinds of grease from the cooking was deposited. This savory compound is called "slush" and is used for lubricating whatever needs to be kept slippery about the ship.

"Wash 'em in that," he said.

I followed his directions and soon had my hands comparatively free from tar except what was deposited under the fingernails. But the natural hue of the skin was gone, to reappear no more for many months. The process of discoloration commenced with a pale yellow, which had gradually deepened, before I finally ceased to dabble in tar, to a rich mahogany.

Jack's attentions continued, and he also constituted himself my champion and defender against the petty tyrannies of the forecastle. On the only occasion when this function became seriously necessary, he performed it with promptness and vigor. It was the custom of the bullies of the forecastle—every large ship's crew has them—to compel the boys to wait on them.

One evening at supper the man who had elected himself autocrat of the starboard watch and was in the habit of vindicating his claim to that distinction by an unusual amount of loud talk, swagger, and swearing, tossed his empty tea pot across to me and said, "Here you, boy, take that to the galley and bring me my tea, and be quick about it."

I had made up my mind to resist the first attempt to order me about and this was my opportunity. I picked up his tin pot and walked deliberately over and set it down beside him on his sea chest and then going back to my place turned facing him and made this speech.

"I might as well tell you, Tom, and all you men right now as any other time that I am not going to take any orders in this ship from anybody but the officers. I don't want to put on any airs. I am just a green boy before the mast and nothing else, and don't know much sailing. I mean to do my duty as well as I can and be a good shipmate. There is nothing any of you will ask me to do, that I won't do to oblige you if I can, but I won't be bullied by anybody, even if you lick me within an inch of my life."

For a minute Tom was paralyzed with amazement. A declaration of independence by a green boy in a ship's forecastle was something quite outside his experience. By the time my speech was finished, however, he had pulled his wits together and started for me with horrible curses and fists doubled up. Jack was on his feet quick as a flash, with his sturdy body between me and Tom.

"Keep your dirty hands off that boy, and stop your ugly jaw," shouted Jack. It looked as if there would be a fight, but just then a big, good-natured sailor put himself in Tom's way and quietly said, "Sit down, you brute."

Tom, like bullies generally, was a coward at heart, with no love for battle except with heavy odds in his favor. To domineer over a boy and thrash him was about the measure of his valor. He had no stomach for Jack and the big sailor. He stopped short in his wild rush for me, and when half a dozen other voices from different parts of the forecastle joined in the verdict—"The boy is right, let him alone"—there was general applause. Tom retired to his chest, grumbling but subdued. His final remark was something about "them gentlemen's sons chewing up dictionaries ashore and coming aboard ship to spit them out in the forecastle."

I never had any more trouble. I kept my promise, by never letting an opportunity go by to do a kind and obliging thing. My determination not to be bullied or ordered about was respected, and throughout the remainder of the voyage I was well treated by every man of the crew, and rather petted and favored in many ways by the best-natured of them.

A few days after this incident, my opportunity came to retaliate on Tom. He had a fearful attack of inflammatory rheumatism. Dissipation on shore and exposure at sea had made him, with all his bravado and outward appearance of strength, but little better than a physical wreck.

One night, in the middle of our watch below, he woke the whole forecastle howling with pain. There were a number of responses more forcible than polite, as, one after another, the sleeping men awoke to a consciousness of where the noise came from that was disturbing their slumbers. I got out of my bunk and went over to Tom's and asked what was the matter. A torrent of curses, mixed with groans and yells, was his only response.

By watching his hands as they went, with spasmodic jerks corresponding to each fresh groan, from one part of his writhing body to another, I made out the localities of the pains, and divined the cause. Then I began to rub him vigorously in the regions indicated, applying some of the contents of a bottle of liniment that I had transferred, with some other personal effects, from the trunk I had brought from home. In half an hour he had become comparatively quiet, apparently much relieved. By this time the cook had got his galley fire going for breakfast. I begged from him some vinegar and salt, and, putting them together in a tin basin, I heated the mixture scalding hot on the galley stove and went back to Tom.

I found him lying on his stomach still groaning and cursing at intervals. Before he knew what I was up to, I stripped his back bare. I poured a lot of the hot salt and vinegar over him, and commenced rubbing it in with all my might. He squirmed and kicked and howled and swore. All the noise he had made before was like the purring of a kitten compared with what now filled the forecastle. But I had him at a disadvantage. Holding him down with one hand gripping the back of his neck, and applying the hot mixture with the other, I gave him no quarter. The men leaned out of their bunks to see what was going on, and laughed or cursed, according to the way the performance struck them. Some seemed to think I was killing him, others that he was killing me. The majority took it as a good joke.

"Give it to him, boy, but don't kill him."

"Serves the ugly cuss right."

"Finish it, boy, and stop his wind, so a fellow can sleep."

One fellow at the far end of the forecastle, only half awake, whose perceptions of the cause of the commotion were rather hazy, murmured dreamily, "The cook is sticking a pig, mates. Fresh pork for breakfast in the cabin."

Meanwhile, Tom was growing more quiet. My vigorous treatment was easing his pain. The fumes of the hot vinegar soothed him, and in half an hour he was sleeping sweetly as an infant. When the watch was called at eight bells, Tom awoke, and surprised to find himself comparatively free from pain, turned out with the rest. He said nothing, and seemed to take no notice of me before the men, but later on, when we were alone on the topgallant forecastle, he suddenly thrust out his tarry hand and said, "Call it square, boy, and when you want anything of Tom Perkins, say the word." That was all. He continued to be the head growler of the starboard watch and to bully whomever he could. But to me, from that time on, he was gentle as a lamb, and showed his rough gratitude in many ways.

The fourth mate, not a bad-natured man at heart, but a little rough, being a hustler himself, wanted to see everybody else hustle. He had an idea that he could impart something of his own surplus vitality to others through his mouth and his muscles. He had a way, therefore, when it was necessary that things should be lively, of accompanying his orders with rather vigorous language and an occasional push in the direction in which he wanted you to go. He prided himself on never striking a man: he only "shoved him," as he would explain when called to account by his superiors. I had a great admiration for this fourth mate physically. I loved to watch him when topsails were being reefed, sitting astride a yardarm and shouting orders to the men on the yard, his jauntily knotted black neckerchief fluttering in the wind, every motion of his body and every tone of his voice indicating that he was heartily enjoying the excitement and danger.

When, however, his magnificent physique and his abounding vitality expressed themselves in shoving me toward some part of the ship where I was wanted in a hurry, and his cheery voice lent its aid in language that I had been taught to consider extremely wicked, I did not admire them so much. One day when he had been particularly active in muscle and prolific of tongue, I came to the conclusion that, audacious as it might seem in a green boy, I must have a private conversation with him. I had too much respect for authority and too much sense of the fitness of things, to say nothing of my respect for the fourth mate's fists in case he should happen to forget himself, to show any insubordination or resentment before the men. A private interview seemed to me altogether the most orderly as well as the safest plan.

That night I watched for my opportunity, and when I saw him alone, leaning over the bulwarks whistling a tune, apparently in excellent humor, I went up to him and said, "Mr. Henry, I would like to speak with you a minute."

"All right, my lad, go ahead. What is it all about?" he answered.

"You see, Mr. Henry, I am no shirk and I don't think I am stupid. I am used to trying to do whatever I have to do as well as I know how and as quickly as I can. I am not a bit hard of hearing and can generally hear what is said to me the first time. I also think I have sense enough to understand what is wanted of me without having it pounded into me. I mean to do my duty in this ship and don't need to have it punched or pulled or cussed into me. They have christened me 'Boy Hatch,' which is a good enough name, and I am satisfied with it and ready to answer to it every time. I don't think it needs any handles to it in front or rear."

"Forward or aft, boy, forward or aft," he put in. "Don't talk sojer talk aboard ship!"

"Forward or aft," I repeated after him, accepting the correction. "Now, Mr. Henry, there isn't any use in shoving me about or swearing at me or giving me a lot of extra names, and... and..." I added in a burst of boyish confidence, "I wish you wouldn't."

During this speech he looked at me very much as he might have done at some new or strange kind of fish that he had hooked up from the deep. I was evidently a marine curiosity to him.

"Well, boy," he said, "that's a very pretty speech, very pretty, and I am not going to punch your head for saying it, as some ship's officers might. I guess you're all right and you and I will be good friends."

"Thank you, Sir, good night," I said, touching my cap.

The fourth mate did not shove me or swear at me or call me names any more after that, and I took particular pains to please him by jumping about in as lively a manner as I could whenever he spoke to me.

It was shortly after this that I was transferred to the port, or chief mate's, watch. Jack was as uneasy as an old hen robbed of her brood. He fluttered about the port forecastle when it was our watch below and his on deck to see that nothing went amiss with me among my new watch mates, and spent more than half his own time when his watch was below, hovering near me on deck. After two or three days of this, I noticed that Jack became very much preoccupied in mind and serious of face, as if planning something important.

One afternoon I saw him go up to the chief mate and salute in man-of-war fashion. This salute, accompanied with a peculiar but indescribable air of humility, were accomplishments brought over from his man-of-war life, which he brought into use when he wanted to be particularly deferential to an officer of whom he was about to ask a favor. He had a notion that mates in merchant ships, where this sort of ceremony is not enforced, rather liked it, and he played it for all it was worth when he had a purpose to accomplish. I noticed that he was particularly impressive on this occasion. I was too far away to hear what passed between them, but I thought the mate looked my way once or twice with a queer smile on his face. Presently Jack saluted again and left the mate. He maintained his deferential air, and his dignity, until he had a deck house between himself and the mate, when he came to me with a lively selection of steps out of the Sailor's Hornpipe and said, "I've fixed it."

"What have you fixed, Jack?" I asked.

"Got m'self exchanged into the port watch, all on your account, young feller," he answered. I was glad, for I had missed Jack.

In the first dog watch that night, Jack transferred his green chest to the port forecastle, and Bill Jones, a smart sailorman but not an overly agreeable shipmate, went over to the starboard. A good-natured sailor, whose bunk was under mine, gave it up to Jack and took the one vacated by Bill. So our relative positions in the forecastle were re-established, to Jack's immense satisfaction and mine.

The next day I had my first experience of going aloft—not

very much aloft it must be confessed, but it was a beginning.
My most serious misgivings concerning the sort of figure I
should cut as a sailor had been on this point. I had never had
much nerve for climbing or lofty and perilous exercises of any
kind. My reputation among my youthful playmates for either
boldness or skill in climbing trees or flagstaffs or walking along
the ridgepoles of barns was not brilliant.

During my first day or two aboard the ship, I had watched the
men aloft on the higher yards with something like awe, and had
wondered whether it was possible that I could ever come to feel
at ease up there. Whenever a royal was clewed up and one of the
mates called out "A couple of you jump up there and furl that
royal," I would feel the cold chills running down my back, with
the fear that he might single me out and order me by name to
go. I did not see how I could do it; yet I felt all the time an
ambition to do it, and had made up my mind not to flinch when
the time came.

Now, we had been at sea nearly a week and I was well on my
sea legs. When I had overcome the exhaustion of the first few
days of unaccustomed toil and exposure, and had begun to feel
an invigoration before unknown, I felt ashamed of being of no
use above the deck, and humiliated to think that my never having been ordered aloft was an indication that I was considered
of no account in the more important part of a sailor's duties. I
envied the other boys when I saw them scampering like monkeys up the rigging, and watched them clinging to the yards as
the tall masts swung with the rolling of the ship like inverted
pendulums across the sky.

My transfer to the port watch had brought me under the eye
of the big third mate when on deck, and he had set me to do
almost everything that a green boy could do about a ship, except
to go aloft. I saw him one day, looking up at the cross-jack yard,
then around the deck, and then up at the yard again. Following

his look, I saw that one of the gaskets of the furled mizzen course was flying loose, and guessed that he wanted someone to go up and make it fast. The crew were all busy forward or serving and parceling the rigging aloft except the man at the wheel.

"May I go up and fix it, Sir," I said, going up to him and pointing to the flying rope.

"Yes, go ahead, but look out for yourself," he answered good-naturedly.

I climbed upon the rail, went cautiously up the mizzen rigging to the level of the cross-jack yard. I had some difficulty in transferring my feet from the shrouds to the foot rope under the yard, but succeeded at last; and crept carefully along to where the loose gasket was fastened to the yard. Then I wound it around the yard and sail, as I saw the others were, made it fast and came down.

The third mate had kept his eye on me, and when I swung myself from the rail to the deck, he smiled encouragingly as much as to say "Very well done for the first time."

That night when we were on deck in the middle watch and I saw the third mate standing by himself near the main rigging, I went up to him and ventured to ask, "Mr. Sargent, what is the reason you have never ordered me aloft until I asked you today to let me go?"

"Sit down here on this spare topsail yard, and I will tell you why," he said, his rough voice softened by a touch of gentle sadness that I had never heard in it before. We sat down, and after a moment of silence, he began.

I had a young brother once and was very fond of him. When he was about fourteen, I was at home away up in Maine for a few days after a long voyage to the East Indies. I was before the mast then. He wanted to go to sea. We were a race of sailors, and it was in his blood I suppose.

My father had been drowned at sea. My two older brothers were sailors like myself and my mother seldom saw or heard from any of us, for we were not great letter writers. She lived in constant dread of see- ing a sea chest, with the name of one of us painted on it, come home some day with a short message from owner or officer or shipmate, "Lost over- board and drowned from the ship on the_____of _____, 18__" or "died of fever at_____" or to hear that the ship in which one of us had last sailed had gone down in a hurricane with all hands, or had sailed from such a port on such a date and had never been heard of again.

She had hoped to keep the youngest at home with her and to see him take to some way of livelihood on shore that would not be so full of ter- rors for her.

On this visit home, the lad told me of his longing for the sea, and Mother told me how she wanted to keep him by her in her old age. I was young and reckless then, and made light of the dangers of the sea and of my mother's fears.

She reminded me of our father, but I turned it off by saying that he would probably have died just the same if he had stayed ashore. At that time I was a bit of a fatalist, or whatever you may call it, and used to say that there were as great dangers on land as on the sea. I believed then that when a man's time came he would part his cable and ground on the eternal shore, whether he was aboard ship or in his bed at home. This kind of talk encouraged the boy and made him more eager than ever for the excitement and adventure of a sailor's life, but it did not convince Mother.

The result of it all was, that with many misgivings and tears, and with many traces on her face in the mornings of sleepless nights of weep- ing and praying, she reluctantly consented to let him go away with me, on the solemn promise that I would keep him with me and look after him.

"Never fear, Mother, but I will bring him back to you safe and sound," was my lighthearted but foolhardy exclamation when it was finally settled. Poor Mother! Her only consolation in the sorrow of it all to her was that he was going with me, for, reckless and devil-may-

care as I was, sailor-like, I had always been a good son to her; and I loved her and the boy, and she knew it.

Well, we went away, and shipped together in a barque bound to Valparaiso, I as an A.B. and he as boy. The mate of the barque was an ugly, unfeeling brute, but he treated the boy decently. I suppose he had seen that it would be safer for him to fool with a tiger's cubs in a jungle than to lay his hands to that boy when I was around.

One night when I was sick in the forecastle, we ran into a gale and all hands were called to shorten sail. I was uneasy about the boy on deck in that wild night without me, but there was no help for it. When all had been made snug, and the watch came below I looked for him among the men as they came down the forecastle ladder, dripping with wet, but in unaccustomed silence. When the last man had come down and pulled the slide over the forecastle hatch, the trim little figure I was looking for was nowhere to be seen.

The men seemed to avoid looking at me, and turned their backs toward me as they pulled off their oilskins and boots. A horrible thought suddenly seized me, and springing from my berth, forgetful of sickness and of everything but the one idea that completely possessed all my faculties for the moment, I furiously grabbed the first man I came to and shook him till his teeth chattered, exclaiming fiercely.

"What has become of that boy? Tell me quick before I choke the life out of you." The other men gathered around.

"Steady there, shipmate. How can we tell you anything and you raging like a wild beast," said one. "Be quiet now and we'll try to make the best of a bad job," put in another.

Then they told me what they knew, and putting it all together with what I learned afterwards, this is what had happened.

When the topgallant sails were clewed up and the topsail yards lowered away, the men were ordered aloft to furl and reef. The boy, not knowing what was expected of him, stopped on deck when the others jumped into the rigging.

The mate ordered him to get up there with the rest, and when, con-

fused and terrified, the boy hesitated for a moment, the mate had seized a rope's end and driven him into the main rigging and up the slippery shrouds. One of the men had seen this, and told me of it, with curses on the mate. No more was thought of the boy, and he was not missed until they were down on deck again hauling on the topsail halyards. Then someone asked, "Where is the boy?" No one had seen him after they got out on the yards.

One man who had been on the topsail yard thought he had seen a dark object flying through the air as a flash of lightening gleamed for a second. Another had thought he heard something like a faint cry to leeward, but concluded it was only the creaking of a block.

I saw it all now. We had been out only a few days. The boy had never been aloft except once or twice with me in fine weather. He did not know how to handle himself in the rigging in storm and darkness. This was his first experience of a wild night at sea. He was no coward, it wasn't in his blood to be a coward. But he had been dazed and bewildered, and I was not there to tell him what to do. No one else had taken any notice of him in the hurry and confusion of getting sail off the ship except that cursed mate who had rope-ended him aloft. He had tried to get up to the topgallant yard, I suppose, and had fallen from the rigging or to crosstrees in a weather roll of the ship and gone overboard. Not being missed till the men were all on deck again, no cry of man overboard had been raised. No effort had been made to save him.

I was wild with rage and excitement. I made a dash for the forecastle ladder, swearing that I would cut the heart out of that mate. The men held me back. I fought like a madman with the strength of delirium, but they were too many for me and succeeded at last in getting me into my bunk. This they told me afterward, for I remembered nothing after the first wild whirl of grief and rage.

I was delirious with fever for three weeks. When I came to my senses, I found that the mate had left the ship at Rio. It was well for both of us that he did.

I never had the heart to write home and tell Mother what had hap-

pened. I felt as though I could never look her in the face again. It was a relief to me when I heard a year later on my return from that unlucky voyage that she had died peacefully without knowing it. I couldn't help feeling that it was better for her to find it out up there than in this world.

Now, boy, you understand why, since I have been an officer, I have never sent a green boy aloft until he was ready to go.

The moon just then came out of a cloud that had obscured it while he was telling me this story; and as I looked at his face it was turned up to the sky, and something was glistening on his weather-beaten cheek. It was then that I found out how tender the heart was that beat under that rough exterior.

Chapter Three ↝

My progress in seamanship from this time on was rapid. I seized every opportunity to go aloft and soon found that it was easier than I thought. I became fond of the excitement and exhilaration of it, and felt proud to be among the men on a topsail or topgallant yard, reefing or furling. I sometimes got in their way and received a good-natured punch or curse, which, however, in no wise checked my ambition or disturbed my enjoyment of the feeling that I was really becoming a sailor.

In all this, Jack was my constant attendant and indefatigable tutor. He had come to feel a sort of proprietorship in me and in my nautical accomplishments that made him prouder of them than even I could be myself. He was a thorough sailor, every inch of him, and what he could not teach one about sea lore and sailor craft would not be worth knowing. He was by long odds the best all-around seaman in the ship and was so recognized by officers and men alike. He was appreciated by the former and respected by the latter. His man-of-war training had made him an uncompromising stickler for orderliness and discipline. He had no use for a shirking sailor or for a clumsy or shiftless piece of sailor work, and he made no bones of expressing his contempt for either. "You orter be ashamed o' yersel' for sich a lubberly piece o' parcelin' as that," he would say to some bungling or careless shipmate. "If this 'ere boy as hain't been aboard ship but a couple o' weeks yet, couldn't do a better job, I'd cuss m'self for wastin' time on 'im an' begin ter larn seamanship ter that thar big black 'og in the pen forward." And his blunt criticisms were seldom resented.

Some amusing things happened through my want of experience and lack of knowledge to match my zeal. One day I was sent up to slush the fore topgallant mast. I filled my slush bucket at the barrel that stood just outside the cook's galley, and went gaily to my task. The weather was fine and bracing, just a fresh breeze blowing, and the sun shining brightly. I made my way up the topgallant rigging to the masthead, made my bucket fast by its lanyard to a backstay with a slipknot so that I could move it along down as I worked from the masthead downward, and went at it. I had but just begun, when, as I was reaching to the bucket for a handful of slush, it suddenly disappeared. Looking downward, I saw it sliding swiftly down the backstay. It fetched up on the rail with a bang, going all to pieces and scattering its contents over deck and bulwarks. I had not made my slip knot right, and it had slipped prematurely on its own responsibility without any help from me.

Luckily the chief mate was on the poop aft, intent on taking the sun, and the third mate and most of the watch were busy at something on the forecastle forward. I succeeded in getting down on deck, securing another bucket, filling it, and getting back to my post of duty without attracting attention except from old Duffy the cook, who remarked with a grin that perhaps I had better take the barrel along with me at once and be done with it if I was going to slush the whole ship.

This time I made out to keep my bucket from going down any faster than I did. When I had, as I supposed, sufficiently slushed the mast, I went down on deck. I met the third mate going aft. He stopped and looked me over and laughed.

"What have you been doing, boy?" he asked.

"Slushing the fore topgallant mast, Sir," I replied, proud as a drum major.

"What were you slushing mostly, the mast or yourself?" he asked.

I knew that I was pretty well covered with the stuff, but had supposed that was a necessary incident to the occupation of slushing a mast in a fresh breeze.

"Suppose you try the weather side next time," he said, and turned away with a fresh laugh. I had gone up on the lee side of the mast and slushed against the wind, with the result that most of what was intended for the mast had been blown back over me. The next time I had to grease a mast, I took Mr. Sargent's advice and went up on the weather side.

When Jack saw me, he almost went into hysterics of laughter, and poked no end of fun at me. After having his laugh out he said, "Come along o' me boy an' fetch yer bucket." He took me up the weather rigging to the main topgallant mast, which also needed slushing, and patiently showed me how it should be done. It is safe to say that there was no more accomplished mast slusher in the ship than I was after he had polished off my education in that branch of sailor learning.

In furling the royals, it was customary in this ship to send two boys, or two of the lightest men, to the fore or main royal yards, while one boy was expected to tie up the mizzen alone. I had seen the other boys do it, and from the deck it looked an easy thing to do. I was ambitious to try my hand at it.

A day or two after the slushing incident, while the ship was carrying all plain sail with the wind abeam, the breeze suddenly freshened and the order came to take the royals in a hurry. The halyards were let go all at once, and, while the men were hauling on the clew lines and bunt lines, the order was given to "lay aloft and furl." I had been on the fore- and main royal yards with another boy or man two or three times, but had never attempted the mizzen alone.

This time I made for the mizzen rigging, and, before any one had noticed me, I was over the top and half-way up the topmast shrouds. There were ratlines on the fore- and main topgallant rigging. On the mizzen there were none, and, from the topmast crosstrees to the topgallant masthead, it was a case of shinning up the two bare shrouds, about eighteen feet. This was an art in which I had as yet no experience or practice.

I did not see just how I was going to do it; but, setting my teeth and gripping the shrouds, I twisted my legs around them, and went at it. When I had got up about six feet I was panting for breath and my arms seemed to be pulling out of their sockets. I had done all my shinning with my hands, lifting my dead weight by main strength, totally ignorant of the part my shins were to perform in the operation. I could hold on no longer, and went sliding down to the crosstrees. Taking breath, I tried again. I got a little higher this time, but was compelled to take another slide. After repeating this performance three or four times, I succeeded at last in reaching the royal yard, breathless, with hands and shins skinless and smarting.

From the deck the mizzen royal looked little more than a small sized tablecloth that a child could handle. Up there, thrashing in the freshening wind, it was quite another affair. I went to work at the bunt, leaving the parts on either side of it flying loose. Then commenced the hardest tussle I ever had in my life. I would get the bunt of the sail well in hand, as I supposed, when a fresh puff of wind, or a roll of the ship, would pull it away from me, and everything would be flying as before. After this had been repeated half a dozen times, and the sail was no nearer being furled than when I first reached the yard, I stopped, to take a breath and consider the situation. By this time the other two royals were furled and the boys were down on the deck.

As I looked down, I became aware that I was the center of

observation to a large part of the watch on deck. The third mate was shouting something to me that, between the roar of the wind and the flapping of the sail, I could not understand. The sail, after bellying out to the breeze, would fly back and bury me in its folds, and several times I thought it would pull me off the yard.

Some of the men were making motions that were unintelligible, and one of the boys, a mischievous monkey of a chap, was making faces at me, and putting his thumb to his nose and wiggling his fingers up at me from the main top. After taking breath, I tackled the sail again. The wind had increased to half a gale. The sea was getting up, and the ship was beginning to pitch and roll in a manner not calculated to increase the comfort or sense of security of a youngster not yet ten days at sea and swinging through the air on a jerking yard with seventy-five or a hundred square yards of canvas flapping viciously around him. After tugging at the bunt awhile, with no better success than before, I suddenly thought if I could only contrive to keep the rest of the sail quiet for a few minutes, I could handle it. Then I crept out on the lee yardarm, and, shaking out the gasket, wound it loosely around the sail and yard. I then repeated the operation to windward. Going back to the bunt, I found no difficulty in controlling it, and soon had it snugly, if not artistically, tied up. I had discovered the secret of furling a square sail by one person alone, by first "smothering the yardarms," as it is called, then making up the bunt, and finally rolling up the sail on the yard, winding the gaskets tight around it and making them fast. Having finished the latter operation, I went down on deck. I had been half an hour doing what I afterwards learned to do in ten minutes.

It was not very scientifically done, the furled sail looking bunchy and uneven in spots, but I felt quite proud to have done it at all without help or instruction. Jack informed me that it was a wonderful performance for a boy but little over a week at sea, and I was very willing to believe him. He accompanied his complimentary remarks with the blunt reproof, "Ye orter asked me about it an' let me told ye how ter do it. Don't ye try none o' them lubberly monkeyshines ag'in 'ithout larnin' from them as knows."

"But I had no time," I answered. "If I had stopped to ask questions some other boy would have got there ahead of me and I wouldn't have had a chance to do it at all."

My blistered hands and raw shins bore testimony to the fact that furling the mizzen royal alone was not the child's play for me that it afterwards became. I was gratified to see that my pluck and persistence in sticking to that royal until I mastered it had raised me materially in the estimation of my shipmates, notwithstanding the fun they made over it at my expense.

About this time I began to have my first experience in steering the ship, by being sent when occasion required to the lee wheel. It was the custom in heavy weather, or when the ship was running dead before the wind, to send a boy to help the man at "taking the lee wheel." The lee wheel was the boy's school for learning to steer. When it was Jack's trick at the wheel, and there was any excuse for help, he always asked for me. He was an excellent steersman and I could have had no better tutor. As Jack considered me an apt pupil, it was a happy time for both of us when circumstances brought us together in that relation.

It was in this connection that I learned how thoroughly Jack was imbued with the traditional superstition of the sailor. We had as second cabin passengers two sisters returning home to visit their parents in England, after several years' sojourn in America. They were English women of the middle class, but with more than ordinary intelligence and refinement. I used to hear them, as they sat together on deck on sunny days, talking over the anticipated pleasure of once more seeing home and friends.

On the thirteenth day after leaving New York, one of them, after a brief illness, died. The grief of the survivor was pathetic. She sat all day tearless beside the dead, never speaking a word, and scarcely making a movement. It seemed as though the circumstances of her bereavement, the homeward-bound journey, the eagerness with which they had looked forward to the greetings that awaited them, the anticipated pleasures which they were to share together, and the association of every expected joy, made the sorrow more intense than if it had come before the journey commenced. The pleasure with which she had looked forward to the hour when they should together catch the first sight of their native land, was now turned into an awful dread. The rosy visions of joyful greetings had become to her nightmares of sorrow and mourning. All hope and life seemed to have died out of her. She begged hard as night approached that her sister's body might be carried home and not committed to the pitiless sea, there to find an unmarked grave in its fathomless depths, that the kind-hearted captain yielded to her entreaties, and promised to comply with her wishes if wind and weather would permit.

That night a platform was prepared in a boat which was hung from temporary davits at the ship's stern by laying planks fore and aft across the thwarts. The body was laid on it and covered with canvass. The weather was now cold, and the wind fair and blowing fresh. It was hoped that if these conditions continued for three or four days, we might reach Liverpool before decomposition set in.

At four bells in the middle watch (two o'clock a.m.), it was Jack's trick at the wheel, and I was with him. The night was dark; the ghostly glimmer of the phosphorescent waves diffused an unearthly suggestion of light, which yet was not light; the masts and sails loomed in the darkness like the dim and shifting outlines of exaggerated specters; the sound of the wind in the rigging was weird and melancholy. I noticed that Jack's glance wandered over his shoulder oftener than it sought the compass in the binnacle. I had to tell him several times, "We're off the course, Jack."

The silent and motionless thing under the canvas a few feet behind us seemed to have a fascination for him, while it filled him with dread. His grasp on the wheel, usually so firm and steady now seemed nerveless and uncertain. Much of the time I found that I was virtually steering the ship alone.

Death was no unfamiliar thing to Jack. Without a shudder he had helped to sew up in their canvas coffins the mangled bodies of shipmates, and to tip the hatch cover from which they slid to their long sleep at the bottom of the sea. But, on this weird night, the still form of a frail woman, the outlines of which were dimly seen at intervals against the glimmering wake of the ship, was another thing, and its proximity unnerved him.

Suddenly I felt the whole weight of the wheel in my own grasp with a force that taxed all my strength. I looked where Jack had stood. The faint gleam of the binnacle lamp shone on the spokes where his hands ought to be, but they were not there. I felt for him with my feet, not daring to take a hand off the wheel for a second. I felt only empty air; Jack was gone.

Finding that I was really steering the ship, I instinctively shifted my position from the lee to the weather side of the wheel, which brought me where Jack had stood, and made my range of vision what his had been. Then I saw, as if rising out of the deck to leeward, and gliding slowly toward the stern, the semblance of a human figure, faintly outlined in the obscurity by the white drapery that seemed to float about it. It might well have been taken for the spirit of the dead woman coming back to the form to which it had once given life.

My hair seemed standing on end. My hands shook so that if it had not been that the strain was off the wheel for the moment, I should have lost all control of it. My knees seemed to give way under me. I did not believe in ghosts, and in an instant it flashed across my mind that it was the living sister, not the dead one, who walked abroad in the darkness. It was fortunate that I recovered my senses and the control of my muscles just as the next effort of the ship to broach caught the rudder with a force that required all my strength on the wheel to meet it and hold her steady.

I watched the figure as it reached the stern rail and, kneeling on it, leaned forward over the general gunwale of the boat. I dared not cry out for fear that, startled by my voice, she might fall into the sea. Her position was perilous at best, for the swaying of the boat as the ship rose and fell, might pull her overboard at any moment.

While I was sorely perplexed, between my responsibility for steering the ship and my anxiety for the woman, the third mate suddenly appeared at my side. The flapping of the sails, caused by my uncertain steering, had attracted his attention, and he had come to see what was the matter at the wheel. By the light from the binnacle he saw that I was alone. Fearing that he would call out for a man to come aft, I touched his arm and pointing to the woman, gave him a warning hush. He took in the situation at once, and, seizing the wheel himself, said to me, "Take care of the woman and then send a man aft to me."

I approached her cautiously, and, laying my hands gently but firmly on her shoulders in a way to prevent her from falling between the stern rail and boat if startled, I said quietly, "You should not be out here in this dress. You will take cold and be sick; and then who will attend to your sister's body when we get in?"

She neither moved nor spoke nor looked at me, but just leaned her head on the gunwale of the boat, with one arm stretched out so that it touched the canvas covering the body. I thought she was dazed with grief and chilled with the cold. I put one arm around her, and, taking hold of her hand, raised her gently as I could to her feet. She yielded without resistance and followed me unhesitatingly as I led her by the hand across the deck and down the four or five steps that led from the poop to the main deck, then along to the companionway leading to the second cabin. As we went down the stairs and came under the light of the lamp burning just outside the cabin door, I turned and looked at her. Her eyes were closed. Her features were motionless, and her face wore a peaceful expression, quite different from what I had expected to see. She was walking in her sleep.

I woke the second cabin stewardess who was dozing just inside the cabin door, and, explained to her the situation, to get the sleeping woman into her berth without waking her if possible. Then I went on deck and finding Jack sitting silent and grave on the spare spars under the lee bulwarks told him the third mate wanted him at the wheel.

"Is it gone boy?" he asked with a tone such as one might use in a graveyard at night.

"Is what gone, Jack?

"IT."

"Yes, Jack, IT has just gone back to bed in the second cabin."

Jack had risen from his seat and started aft.

"Come with me, boy, you know it is your trick at the lee wheel."

I followed him. When we reached the wheel the third mate relinquished it to Jack with a few words about the course, and not a syllable to indicate that anything unusual had happened any more than if Jack had simply relieved him at the wheel in the usual way. He left the poop and resumed his walk on the lee side of the quarterdeck.

The first mate, pacing the weather side, had taken no further notice. After saying to the third mate ten or fifteen minutes before, "Mr. Sargent, the topsails are shaking, go and see if the man at the wheel is asleep, and tell him to mind his weather leeches," he found in a few minutes that the sails were full and the ship steady.

When Jack and I were alone, I told him all about it, and rallied him on his superstitious fears.

"You can make fun o' me if you like, boy, but who wants ghosts' company at th' wheel in a dark night."

"Nonsense, Jack, there are no ghosts."

Solemnly wagging his head from side to side several times before speaking, he said at last, "Howsomever it may be where ye come from boy, I don't presume t' say, it so bein' as I never cruised in them latitudes, but I tell ye sonny, thar' be ghosts at sea—I've seen 'em."

I tried several times after this to beguile Jack into telling me a genuine sea ghost story out of his own experience, but I could never lead him any further in that direction than to solemn repetitions of the foregoing statement.

Somehow the story leaked out in the forecastle—I don't know how for I had never mentioned it—and it brought up one night the subject of ghosts. There were a variety of opinions. The forecastle, like the club and the forum, has its agnostics, though probably in much smaller proportion. If you should call them by that name aboard ship they would not know what you meant, and would resent it as an epithet of opprobrium and tell you to "stop y'r jaw."

The majority of sailors are naturally religious in sentiment, though they may be far from it in practice. They are firm believers in the supernatural, both divine and diabolical. To them, both God and the devil are personal realities. There are a few, however, who, like their skeptical brethren ashore, believe in nothing that cannot be seen or handled or demonstrated to the senses and the reason.

In our forecastle, a small minority scouted ghosts. The

majority believed in them. Neither party would have attempted to give any logical reasons for their beliefs or unbeliefs. Several believed firmly that they had seen them. The discussion did not run much to argument. It was a matter of personal experience.

One man told how, aboard a ship in the China Sea, he had once dreamed that he was at home and that his mother died. Lying awake after his dream, thinking about it, he suddenly saw his brother, who had been drowned at sea several years before, standing by his berth, his hair and clothes dripping with wet, and heard him say distinctly, "Ben, our mother died an hour ago, an' I've come to tell you." The man continued: "Afore I had a chance so much as to ask 'im wot the old lady died of, or to say, 'How are you, Tom, and how's the weather where yer livin' now,' he seemed to kind o' melt away through the side o' the ship out o' sight." He then told how the next day he got the mate to figure out for him the latitude and longitude where the ship was at the time of his dream and to tell him what time it was at two o'clock that morning at the place in England where his mother lived, and put it down with the date on a piece of paper, which he carefully preserved. At the end of the voyage, he went home and found that his mother had really died at the time corresponding with that of his dream.

One of the unbelievers in ghosts expressed his opinion in this way: "Ye see, mate, ye was a-dreamin' all the time, and when ye thought you seen that brother o' yern, you was sleepin' like a hinfant and didn't know it."

The other stoutly contended that this could not have been because, to quote his own words, "I had woke up after the dreamin' and feelin' a bit out o' sorts, I turned out for a turn on deck and a pull at my pipe. I had only jes' turned in agin, when Tom showed his self, and how do you make it out about the old lady dyin' just the time I was dreamin' about her?" No one attempted an explanation of this part of the mystery, and it remained unsolved.

It is characteristic of sailors' ghosts that they usually make their appearance in a manner suggestive of the circumstances of their death, which accounts for the dripping hair and clothes in which the ghost of Ben's drowned brother presented itself. Another related how on his last voyage, a man fell from the top-gallant yard to the deck, and, as he expressed it, "Mashed his carcass into a jelly, without a whole bone left in it." He had been a silent man, who said little, and no one knew his real name, or where he came from.

"The next night," the narrator went on, "while eight bells was strikin' at the end of the middle watch, I was on the to'gal'nt yard makin' all snug after furlin' and my mate had gone down, when all at once I see another man just to windward of the bunt of the sail lookin' like he was hangin' on by the gaskets, 'tho I couldn't rightly see what he had a hold of. He seemed kind o' limp, and happenin' to look down, I see his feet wa'n't on the foot ropes, but just hangin' loose like, and swingin' with the roll and pitch of the ship. First I thought it was my mate come up agin, and I asked him what for. He didn't answer, and when I took another look, the thing was a sittin' 'stride the yard, leanin' agin' the mast, only kind o' doubled up. After a bit, his hand begun to move along the after side of the yard, clear of the sail, and I noticed he was writin' some'at with his finger, and it looked like where you've scratched a lucifer match in the dark that didn't light. The letters kind o' waved back'ard and for'ard and came and went, and 'twas a minute or so afore I could see what they spelt. Then it came out clear for a second, and this was it:

> *James Collins*
> *10 Waterloo Road*
> *Liverpool*

The narrator illustrated the appearance of the writing with a pencil on the back of an old letter, that he fished out of his bunk, something like the above.

"I was near fallin' off the yard with the turn it gi' me," he continued, "and a minit after, when the thing kind o' faded away in a sort o' blue mist, I slid down to the deck as white as the queen's pocket han'kerchief and tremblin' like a jellyfish. Then I took a pull on my brain tackle and got my wits steady. I told my shipmates about it, and we talked it over in the fo'cs'le and settled it that the writin' meant we was to send his chest to that place. The cur'us thing about it was, there warn't a scratch of a name or place on his chest or any of his fixin's. When we got to Liverpool, two of us went to the place he had wrote on that to'-gal'nt yard, and found a widder woman hangin' out there as had a son named James Collins, gone to sea, and hadn't been heard of for six year.

"I s'pose" he concluded, "the poor chap when he went so sudden, called to mind his name had been *Jack Carlin* on the articles. An' nuthin' to show who he was or where he belonged, was feared his old mother'd never see his dunnage, draw his pay, or know where he'd fetched up. So he got half an hour's leave from whatever sailors paradise he'd gone to an' come and tol' me about it."

"Why didn't he talk it right out like Ben's brother here, and not go foolin' round a to'gal'nt yard with brimstone matches when he was like to set the ship afire may be?" asked one of the unbelievers.

"You see, mate," was the ready answer, "I suppose when he fell from aloft, he most likely struck on his head an' knocked his jaw tackle all out o' shape, so he couldn't talk, an' that finger he wrote with was, maybe, the only thing he had about him that warn't busted." The skeptic, with an incredulous smile, looked around the circle of crouching figures puffing at their pipes as they leaned forward on their chests under the smoky light of the forecastle lamp, as if to appeal to them to take notice of the ridiculousness of this ghostly yarn. But the narrator of it puffed in solemn silence without the twitch of a muscle of his stolid face or the ghost of a twinkle in his eye. Several stories followed, all smacking of one or another of the peculiar and quaint forms and fancies in which the imagination of the sailor clothes his belief in the supernatural.

Chapter Four ✍

The day after the occurrences above related, I was in the main topmast rigging with a sailor named Bob Rogers, helping him with some chafing gear. He was a handsome good-natured fellow whom everybody liked. He was one who always went to sea with a chest full of good sea clothes, wore them jauntily, and was ready to share them with an impoverished shipmate. He was as near to being an ideal sailor of the best type as it was ever my fortune to be shipmates with.

While we were working in the rigging and talking—our conversation consisting mainly of my questions and his answers on nautical matters—a Latin quotation, applicable to something that had been said, and familiar to me, slipped out of his mouth. Looking up at him in surprise, for his talk was ordinarily in the most pronounced sailor dialect without anything to suggest education or culture, I asked him, "What do you know about that, Bob?"

"Perhaps I know more about it than you do," he answered. Whereupon he went on to quote whole passages from the Latin and Greek classics with a fluency and accuracy that would have done credit to a college tutor.

I asked him for an explanation.

"I will tell you all about it tonight," he said, and relapsed into his former forecastle manner, from which he did not emerge again during the completion of our task.

That night in the middle watch, I sought Bob and asked him for his story. Seeking a sheltered spot under the lee of the galley, we sat down on a pile of old sails, and he began.

I am not what I seem. Or rather I <u>am</u> what I seem, but I am something else beside, something entirely different. I have personated the rough and illiterate Jack-tar so long that I sometimes almost forget that he is not my real self, just as I have heard that some actors playing the same parts continuously for long periods, lose their identity in great measure, and come to live and act and talk in everyday life, very much like the characters they represent, on the stage.

My name is Harry Montclair. I was born in the County of_____ on the west coast of England, where my family still lives on a large, well-kept and productive ancestral estate. My father is a country gentleman of the old school, proud and punctilious, jealous of the properties and wedded to the conventionalities of English country life and county social traditions. I do not suppose there is a narrower rut on the face of the earth than that in which our family has run for generations. To violate one of its traditional notions of the fitness of things is worse than to commit a crime. My mother—she is dead now —was a gentle, tender hearted woman who cared more for the love of her children than for all the social luster of her own and my father's families combined. Having but little self-assertion and no taste for contention or resistance, and loving peace and quietness, she lost her individuality in the depressing atmosphere of our house and was decimated by my father's stronger will.

My brothers and sisters, of whom there were six in all, took to the family rut as naturally as the young ducks to the pond in the poultry yard. I was the exception. I was not built to run in a rut. I rebelled against the limitations that our social position and its supposed obligations imposed upon me. I was neither wild nor vicious. I loved what was honorable and virtuous and manly wherever I saw it. I insisted on holding in higher esteem the humblest peasant on the estate who performed a brave and generous act than the man who did a mean and selfish thing though his veins might be swelling with the bluest blood in the United Kingdom. I sought my companions and formed my friendships where I found congenial spirits without regard to the accidents of birth. I treated with undisguised contempt the petty meannesses and the larger vices which found their license in ancestral blood and took shelter behind social position. Finally I performed my crowning act of disloyalty to all that my family held most dear and shocked the whole county by falling in love with the daughter of one of my father's prosperous tenants. She was beautiful, well-educated, and accomplished. Her manners were refined and her character above reproach. She was pious, charitable, and thoroughly good, and was loved and respected by the whole neighborhood. But all these things counted for nothing in comparison with the one supreme requirement which she lacked. She did not have the right sort of blood in the pretty veins whose delicate tracery under the fair skin had such a charm for me.

I was too honest and manly to do anything under cover. Nor would I degrade her or myself by keeping my love for her a secret. I announced it boldly at the breakfast table the morning after we had shown our hearts to each other under the moon and stars. I had expected to stir the blood of all the generations of Montclairs with horror, and I was not disappointed.

My father got red in the face and gasped several times before he could find language strong enough to express his anger and disgust. My older brother looked grave. My two grownup sisters' noses went up in the air. The young ones giggled, and then, with a comic imitation of the expressions on the faces of the others, raised their hands and exclaimed, "Oh, brother Harry." These youngsters, who were not old enough yet to feel the full weight of the family dignity on their young shoulders, loved their brother Harry and his free and easy ways, to say nothing of the toys and candies he used to bring then when he came home for the holidays from Eton and Cambridge. But the family rut was beginning already to close in on their childish feet, and the family blood was beginning to curdle in their warm, young hearts. In the stormy discussion that followed, the play of these conflicting influences in their faces was both pathetic and ludicrous.

I stoutly defended my love on the simple ground of the beauty and excellence of its object, without the slightest expectation that this consideration would have any weight, except with my mother, whom I knew secretly sympathized with me. My sisters knew and respected my love in her place, as they would have put it, but the thought of her as their brother's wife and their social equal was intolerable.

Well, it ended, as I expected it would, by my father declaring that if I married that girl he would disinherit me and would never want to see my face inside his door again. Of course I married her. I took her to London where, through the influence of some of my old college chums, I got a government clerkship on a small salary.

After one happy year in which all our trials and perplexities became trifles, and our little pleasures mountains of joy, she died giving birth to our child.

All my interest and affection then became centered in the little one. In less than two months she followed her mother to the cemetery, and I was left desolate. I resented the invitation received from home to rejoin the family now that she was dead. A home where I was welcome only because she had gone out of my life was no home for me. I rebelled against God for taking away all I had to live for. I became desperate and reckless. I wanted to get away as far away as possible from everything that was associated with my short dream of bliss. I threw up my clerkship and determined to become a wanderer on the face of the earth.

Having no money with which to travel as a gentleman, and being of an adventurous spirit, I naturally turned to the sea. I was then twenty-three years old, strong, robust and in perfect health. I did not want ease or luxury. I wanted hardship and peril, and a life as unlike that I had previously lived as possible. Anything to take me out of myself. I went to Liverpool and shipped before the mast in the first ship that would take me as a green hand. It happened to be a New York packet, a part *of whose crew had deserted. Sailors were scarce, and they ware glad to take anything they could get that promised activity and muscle, without regard to experience. At New York I was paid off and discharged with the rest of the crew.*

I next shipped in an American ship bound for a trading voyage among the islands of the Pacific. We were wrecked on a reef off one of the Sandwich Islands. The ship was a total loss, but all hands got ashore. I made my way to Honolulu, then the principal resort for American whalers in the Pacific. I shipped in one of them and spent two years blubber-hunting in high latitudes. Since then I have sailed all seas, under all flags, and in all sorts of craft, except slavers and pirates. I have been shipwrecked half a dozen times, and have faced danger and death in almost every form. Until two years ago, I lived a reckless dissipated life, participating in almost all the vices common to Jack-tar ashore. Then I wandered one Sunday into the Seamen's Bethel in New York, where I heard something that touched my heart and changed my life. It might be thought that with this change there would have come a desire and purpose to put my talents and education to some better purpose than following the sea before the mast. I have often thought of it, but the roving habit and the love of the sea had become too deeply rooted to be changed in a day. What may come hereafter I don't know.

I went home once, after I commenced my wandering life, but none of them ever knew it. I took my father at his word, and have never darkened his door since he turned me from it, and have never attempted to. If he ever wants me he must find me out and open the door on conditions that do not dishonor my dead wife or deny that I did right in marrying her. I have left traces here and there by which he can find me if he wants to. If his heart should soften in his old age, it should never be on my conscience that I had rendered the wrong irreparable by placing an impassible barrier between us.

Once, on landing in London, I picked up in a tavern where I was staying a daily newspaper printed in a town near home a day or two before, and the first thing my eye lighted on was a notice of my mother's death and an announcement of her funeral on the following day. *Within an hour I was aboard a railway train headed for my native county. I got off at the nearest station to my father's house at midnight and, walking the intervening ten miles, reached the Parish Church soon after daylight.*

I hung around the churchyard, in sight of home, till I saw the funeral procession coming out of the gates, and the bell began to toll. I entered the church and sat down in an obscure corner. When the funeral service was ended and the invitation was given to those who wished to take a last look at the face of the dead, I went forward with the rest. My bronzed face and rough garb secured me against recognition. I might well have been taken for a fisherman from the coast village three or four miles away where my mother was known and loved for her many kindly acts among the sick and afflicted.

As there were a number of fishermen and peasants among the throng that moved with bowed heads and tearful eyes past the coffin, I was not noticed. There were many humble hearts for miles around that had reason to mourn that day, for my mother in her quiet and unobtrusive way had been a ministering angel to her poor neighbors. No one present could have guessed the deeper emotions that stirred my heart as I looked upon the dead face of the one toward whom in my memories of home there had been no bitterness, only tender affection and reverence. I saw my father still cold and stern and self-sufficient, as I remembered him. I wondered if there was a tender spot anywhere in his nature. I saw my brothers and sisters, more or less reflections, all of them, of this hard impassive man who had dominated them and repressed in them everything but a sense of the dignities of their position.

Of course none of then recognized me or suspected my presence, and, after seeing my mother's coffin deposited in the family vault, I slipped away and rejoined my ship in London.

There was a pause, a long-drawn breath with the suggestion of a sigh in it, and then, "Now, boy, you have my yarn. Exit

Harry Montclair. Enter, Bob Rogers. Let's have a smoke." The transition was as sudden as it was remarkable. While he had been telling his story, he was to the ear a refined and educated gentleman. His voice was low and musical, his manner serious, his language polished and grammatical and entirely free from slang or nautical idioms. I had kept my face partly away, fearing that a look at his tarry hands, his weather-stained face and his rough attire would dispel the illusion. When he had finished his story, and uttered the words last quoted, voice, manner, language, all had changed, and once more smacked of the forecastle or the sailor's boarding house. I turned toward him with a start, uncertain whether I should see a scholar in sailor clothes or a Jack-tar in evening dress.

Bob's power of transforming himself at will interested me greatly. I doubt if he exhibited it to anyone else aboard the ship. I never knew him to do so, but with me, when we were alone. It was a common occurrence after this. Neither character seemed assumed or acted. Each in its turn, whenever it suited his fancy to appear in it, seemed for the time to be his real and natural self. He once told me that he thought of himself as two distinct persons who knew each other very well and were good friends. Bob looked up to and respected Harry for his superior intelligence and learning. Harry liked Bob for his simple-hearted manliness, his seamanship, and his cheerful indifference to hardship and deprivation.

I would like to tell the reader what became of him, if I could. I would give a good deal now, after nearly forty-five years, to know myself. Whether Bob is still sailing the sea or sleeping his last sleep enfolded in its bosom or whether Harry is living on the family estate or lying in dignified repose in the family vault, neither you nor I will probably ever know.

Chapter Five ✑

I had left a sweetheart at home and had brought with me a daguerreotype of her in a little red velvet case, which I cherished as something very sacred and precious.

One night when I thought all the men were asleep, I drew it out from where I had hidden it at the back of my bunk, and leaning out toward the forecastle lamp to make the most of its dim light, I took a long loving look at it.

"Well, boy, that's a nice looking gal, I'd like to kiss her myself," came from the adjoining bunk where a sleepless shipmate had been watching my adoring study of the face so beautiful and dear to my boyish eyes and heart.

I was startled at this sudden interruption of the tender current of my thoughts and shocked that their sacred object should be profaned by vulgar eyes and rude speech. I drew back into my bunk as suddenly as a turtle into his shell and thrust the picture under my pillow. Next day the sailor who had been a witness to my midnight devotions told the others about it when we were at dinner, embellishing the story to suit himself

"You see, shipmates, this 'ere boy is a regular Don what-do-ye-call 'im, and has got 'is bunk full o' pictures of pretty gals, and he just dotes on 'em. I catched 'im at it last night in the middle watch, when I was layin' awake with a bustin' toothache which was like to split my bloomin' 'ead open. That's why he looks so pale, mates, he don't git no sleep.

We'll have to give the little cuss some paregoric tonight and put 'im to sleep somewhar whar he can't git at them durned 'garrytypes."

This speech brought out a general demand for a sight of what had such power to rob a sailor boy of sleep. "Let's see that picture gall'ry, boy, we don't set ourselves up for no connissures in this fo'c'sle, but we knows a good thing when we see it, especially if it's a gal," said one.

"Shut up, mates, maybe 'twas his mama's likeness the young chap was lookin' at and p'r'aps he's only homesick," said a good-natured sentimental young tar, who prided himself on his gentlemanly instincts and his knowledge of the finer feelings.

Another rummaged in his chest and brought out a work of art in very high colors representing himself with a pipe in one hand, his other arm around the waist of a blooming lass sitting on his knee. She wore a yellow dress and a bright red bonnet with blue ribbons, and beside them stood a table with two glasses filled with some kind of purple-colored liquor with a straw sticking out of each.

"I don't mind you've got anything to match that, young feller," he said, holding it away at arm's length and looking at it admiringly. "See here, shipmates, you're turning this youngster's face into a biled lobster wi' yer blackuard jaw tackle," said another.

Meanwhile one of the boys had been poking around in my bunk, turning things upside down and making a mess of it generally. "It's all a bloody lie," he said at last. "There's no pictures in his bunk, and I believe Old Barnacles made the whole thing up." This was the pet name that had been bestowed upon the sailor who had betrayed me. The name was suggested by the peculiar texture of the skin of his face, which had the appearance of being covered with scales.

"He swallowed too much of that duff we had for supper last night, an' had a nightmare. He thought he was lookin' at hi'self in a lookin' glass, and took his ugly mug for a purty gal," said the wit of the watch.

"Thar' ain't no danger of anybody takin' your ugly mug for anything purty, if he had a dozen nightmares onto him all at once, leastwise not till you've been holystoned and sandpapered," said Old Barnacles. This was a delicate allusion to the deeply pitted face of the wit, who had had smallpox.

I had felt myself blushing like a girl during this colloquy, and wished I was out of it, but I did not like to run under fire. In the lull that followed Old Barnacles' last shot, I got up and sauntered out on deck with as unconcerned an air as I could assume. I had hidden the daguerreotype in the bosom of my flannel shirt, where I kept it for most of the time after this, never having the heart to let it be seen in the forecastle again, nor daring to trust it to any hiding place that I could find about my bunk.

When I wanted to look at it, which was pretty often, I used to find some excuse for going aloft, where, sitting astride the topgallant or royal yard, or lying flat out of sight in the top, I would take it out and gaze at it to my heart's content with no fear of being discovered except, perhaps, by the "sweet little cherub that sits up aloft and looks out for the life of poor Jack." I did not seem to mind that fabled protector of sailors a bit.

When the men stripped to the waist in pleasant weather for a wash or change of clothing, the forecastle became a picture gallery. Birds, fishes, mermaids, spouting whales, harpooners erect in the bows of whale boats with harpoons poised in air ready to strike, anchors, capstans, steering wheels, mariners' compasses, quadrants, pairs of hearts pinned together with cupid's arrows, crossed oars, gun-rammers, boarding pikes, pistols, cutlasses, coils of rope, flags of all nations, light-houses, spread eagles, union jacks, skull and crossbones, and even crucifixes and Virgin Marys, all figured in this curious collection of pictures, pricked in many colors into canvases of human skin.

There was hardly a man of them but was more or less elaborately decorated. One big fellow had a full-rigged ship depicted on his broad chest, with sails furled and a chain cable coming out of her hawse hole which, after winding around his body, was made fast to an anchor at the small of his back. Another had a ship under full sail across his breast, and a variety of other objects scattered over his body. The first of these works of art required over a year and the other about nine months for their execution, as their proud possessors confided to me.

Numerous less pretentious designs were scattered over arms and bodies. A favorite device was a female figure with skirts spread at an angle resembling an inverted grocer's funnel and arms akimbo, the words, "The girl I left behind me," in a semi-circle over her head. This was generally on the sailor's arm just above the wrist. In one case the young woman had a nosegay in one hand, a sailor in man-of-war clothes standing beside her holding the other hand, the words "Sally and me" in a scroll under their feet, and the "sweet little cherub" smiled down on them from the top of a skysail pole on which he seemed to be spitted, and which had the appearance of growing out of the top of the sailor's head.

One man had a part of a ship's mast, commencing with the crossing of the topgallant yard in the pit of his stomach, and terminating with the trunk at the top of his breastbone, with a pair of signal halyards hung with flags running down his sides.

Jack's body from waist to neck, and his arms from wrists to shoulders, were a study in mosaic, but his particular pride was a man-of-war's top with the inscription, "Maintop of H.M.S. War-Spite" over it, and "John Corbett, Captain," underneath.

Many kind offers were made to tattoo me, with various suggestions of appropriate designs. One man thought a rooster on top of a hen coop would be about the proper thing. Whether this was an allusion to my care of the live poultry on the ship or to the supposed rural character of my occupations before going to sea or as emblematic of myself, he did not explain.

Another, an irreverent old sea dog who, because I did not swear and ventured once to mildly rebuke him for his excessive profanity, concluded that I must be very pious. He remarked that as he didn't see how I was going to get along without my Sunday school teacher, he suggested an angel in sailor clothes with wings and a harp. At the same time he drew on the top of his chest, with a piece of chalk and considerable rude skill, a rough sketch of his idea. Then he said, "When ye git there, boy, an' git then wings glued onto yer, an' begin to touch up that three-cornered fiddle, don't disremember to speak a good word for Bill Somers. He ain't no beauty an' has never been much on sarm singin' an' prayin', an' he couldn't play a harp no more'n a porpiss could box the compass, 'cept maybe 'twere a bit with a Jew's-harp now an' agin. But you can tell the Commodore as how Bill done his duty aboard ship like a man an' never robbed a shipmate of his last plug o' terbacker nor licked a woman." This last was a thrust at a man of the crew who was suspected of having been guilty of these crimes. It was also an epitome of Bill's creed and of his idea of righteousness in a sailor.

I stoutly resisted all attempts to persuade me to have my own antecedents, present virtues, possible appearance in paradise, or any other subject illustrated on my skin, greatly to Jack's chagrin. He became so far indignant at me as to say one night, "Ye see, boy, you'll never be no kind of a sailor if you're goin' to be that squeamish. A sailor without a picture on him is worse'n a bird without feathers, or a yaller whale. It's onatural like."

They went so far as to discuss the propriety of two of them holding me down on the top of a chest, while the artist of the watch pricked something or other into me.

"If it's nothin' more'n his 'nitials, so as we'll know him agin if he's lost overboard an' we fish him up with his pretty head chawed off by a shark," as one of them put it.

I succeeded, however, in keeping my skin from becoming either a picture book or a card of identification, and brought it home without a mark.

Chapter Six ↝

It was the sixth of November when we sailed from New York, and, on the twenty-third, our anchor went to the bottom of the Mersey opposite the Waterloo Dock at Liverpool. We had made the passage in seventeen days, which was remarkably quick time under canvas in those days. The next day we hauled into the dock, and commenced discharging cargo. The Liverpool docks, with their massive granite bulkheads, their tide gates, and the admirable system under which they are managed, are too well known to need any extended description here.

At that time no fires or lights were allowed aboard ship while in dock, and we were all sent to board ashore. The men were sent to sailor boarding houses, but, with kindly regard to our morals, the four boys, including myself, were sent to board with the mates, at a house of a better class.

It will doubtless interest the sympathetic reader to know that we succeeded in keeping the body of the dead girl until we reached port. As soon as we were made fast in the dock, an undertaker was sent for and she was decently prepared for the journey home and for her final resting place in the village churchyard. Two of us were sent with the sister in a carriage, following the hearse, to the Great Northern Railway Station, where she bid us good-bye with a very sad but grateful heart.

I had sailed from New York with no money, except one large

copper cent which I had kept in my pocket for "luck," all the rest having gone, as before related, for my slender outfit.

I went to the captain and asked him if he would advance me a little money, suggesting my watch as security. I then found out, what I had given no thought to before, that my wages were to be six dollars a month. I had not expected anything when I first met the captain on the wharf in New York. I considered so much in the light of a privilege to be taken in the ship on any terms, that I had not mentioned the subject. This seemed to me like so much clear gain.

The captain said he guessed I need not pawn my watch and he would advance me two months pay. So he handed me two gold sovereigns and two silver dollars, which, in comparison with the previous emptiness of my pockets, made me feel like a capitalist.

In an unguarded moment I communicated my good fortune to Jack. He fidgeted about for a while, and then modestly asked me for the loan of half a crown.

"I've no English money, smaller than sovereigns, Jack," I said with an air as if my pockets were full of them. "When I go ashore to dinner I will get one changed, and lend you half a crown."

Jack suggested modestly that he did not like to put me to so much trouble.

"I'm goin' ashore on an errand for the mate," he said. "I'll take the sov'rin an' get it broke an' take out half a crown an' bring ye back the change."

I confidingly passed over one of my precious sovereigns to Jack. I did not doubt his honesty or intention then and never have since. But I did not understand then, as well as I have learned since, how hard it is for the average sailor to pass a bar-room with money in his pocket, or, once started on a spree, to bring himself to and go about on the other tack, while there is a shot in the locker.

Nothing was seen of Jack for three days.

The mates, not knowing the secret of the sovereign, thought he had deserted the ship. I felt confident that it was only a question of how long a sovereign would keep a sailor going among the dives around the Liverpool docks, before Jack would show up.

For three days I kept an anxious lookout for Jack. I searched for him evenings through the resorts frequented by sailors in the neighborhood of the men's boarding houses, but could not find him. The barmaids to whom I gave descriptions of him had all seen him. English barmaids are amiable and obliging creatures, and are almost always willing to accommodate you with the gratifying intelligence that the man you are looking for "was in here only yesterday," but their information is never of much value toward accomplishing the purpose of your search or tracing its object.

On the morning of the fourth day, upon returning to the ship after breakfast, I saw Jack with the sailmaker, overhauling and repairing sails in the gangway between the cook's galley and the fore rigging on the starboard side of the ship. I was overjoyed to see him. In my anxiety about his personal safety during the last day or two of my unavailing search for him, I had forgotten all about the sovereign and its probable fate. If he would only turn up all right, if he had not deserted or got shanghaied or murdered, I was ready to forgive him if he had squandered a dozen of them.

When, on coming up the gangplank to the deck, I discovered Jack, I started quickly toward him. I was interrupted by one of the mates with an order to do some trifling job which detained me for a few minutes.

While I was occupied in this way, I noticed that Jack had suddenly become interested in something aloft, and, when I had finished and started toward him again, he had climbed on the rail and started up the starboard fore rigging. I followed him. I thought he was getting over the ratlines with unusual alacrity, considering that the ship was in dock, and there was no occasion to hurry as if there were sails to be reefed or furled in a squall. I had hardly got into the rigging before he was over the top. I climbed over after him only to see him half way up the topmast shrouds. When he reached the crosstrees, he made a brief pretext of doing something there, but by the time I got there, he was going down on the port side. It had not occurred to me until now that Jack was running away from me. There had been nothing of the appearance of a chase in our movements. Jack seemed to be going aloft in a perfectly natural way to execute some order he had received, while I, anxious to greet him and express my pleasure at his return, had taken a notion to follow him. I now began to suspect the truth with mixed feelings of sorrow and amusement. I noticed that all this time Jack had affected not to see me. While I was below him, his gaze was aloft, now that I was above him, it was intent on the deck.

I followed him down. He had no sooner reached the deck than he apparently discovered something that required his attention somewhere aloft on the main, and he began to ascend the main rigging. We repeated the same performance here, he going up and I after him until he reached the topmast crosstrees, where he crossed over and started down on the opposite side. This time when I reached the crosstrees, instead of following him down the shrouds as before, I caught the topmast back stay and, sliding rapidly down past him, swung myself into the top just as he reached it, and had him fairly treed at last.

"Hello, Jack," I said, holding out my hand, "how are you?"

He hung his head, half turned it aside in a shamefaced way, and put out his hand. I gave it a hearty shake and said I was very glad to see him.

"You don't seem delighted to see me, Jack," I added.

"I've made a babble of your sovereign, boy," was his reply.

"Sit down here in the top and tell me about it," I said.

After some coaxing, he allowed himself to be persuaded, and then told me how he had gone and got the sovereign changed, as he had proposed; how he had taken out a half crown and tied the balance up in a corner of his handkerchief to bring to me; how he had met an old shipmate and treated him out of the half crown; how the old shipmate treated him in return; how a girl came and sat on his knee, when he had to treat her and the old shipmate again; and how the old shipmate had treated him and the girl and so on, until in a confused whirl of old shipmates and girls he had finally lost his bearings altogether; and could give no further account of himself, until he found himself in his bunk aboard the ship that morning with a suit of old clothes in place of his own and his pockets empty.

Jack showed great remorse on account of the wrong he had done me in the matter of the sovereign, and I had much difficulty in comforting him. The fact that he had been shamefully drunk for three days among the vilest dens in Liverpool did not seem to trouble his conscience or disturb his self-respect in the least.

It never seemed to occur to Jack that he could pay me back the money some time. Packet sailors, making these short voyages of from two-and-a-half to three months, were so accustomed to having their month's advance confiscated by the boarding house sharks for real or imaginary indebtedness, and to see the balance, when they were paid off at the end of the voyage, swallowed up in the first week or so of carousing ashore, that it seldom occurred to them that they would ever have any money at their own disposal with which, in their sober senses, to voluntarily pay a debt. It was for this reason, I suppose, that Jack seemed to mourn the loss to me of the squandered sovereign as irreparable. I remembered his deposit in the Seaman's Savings Bank, but as he seemed to be entirely oblivious of it for the moment, I did not mention it.

While in the dock at Liverpool we were kept very busy, the most expert of the sailormen in setting up and renewing standing rigging fore and aft, alow and aloft; reeving new running rigging where required; making and mending sails, etc. The remainder of the crew was busy with handling cargo out and in; keeping the ship in such order as the confusion and litter incident to unloading and loading would permit; scraping spars, scouring, scrubbing and painting. I had a hand in almost everything that was going on.

My brief experience at sea had already invigorated me beyond expectation. I felt full of life and energy, eager to learn, and ambitious to make myself useful and to be reckoned of some account in the ship. When the captain came aboard one day, and, giving me a kindly nod of recognition, complimented me on my improved appearance as to health and my progress and activity in sailor duties, I felt as proud as if I had won a medal of honor.

We had loaded for Liverpool with a two-thirds cargo of cotton, and filled up with a miscellaneous assortment of American products. We had wheat and corn in bags, barrels of flour, hogsheads of leaf tobacco, casks of New England rum and of Kentucky whiskey, barrels of apples, boxes of cheese, agricultural implements, crates of furniture, household utensils, and even maple sugar and cider, together with a variety of other articles which few persons would probably imagine were being transported from the United States to Great Britain in 1849. Sometimes I would be engaged all day in trotting down the gangplank with bags of corn on my shoulders and trotting up again for fresh loads, at other times in rolling barrels, tumbling bales of cotton, or carrying boxes and packages of various kinds. Sometimes I would have a spell in the rigging with the men, and sometimes with the carpenter in the 'tween decks where, as the space was cleared of cargo, he was fitting up bunks and otherwise transforming it into steerage quarters for the emigrants we expected to take to America on the return passage. We knocked off at six o'clock, when I would go to the boarding house, a very tired and hungry, but, on the whole, a very contented boy. I was happy in the consciousness of improving health and strength, and in the sense of achieving success in novel and unaccustomed experiences. In the evenings after supper we boys would sally forth to explore the town.

We were Fred McGilvary, Jack McCann, Jack Ward and myself, known respectively aboard ship as "Boy Fred," "Boy Jack," "Boy Ward," and "Boy Hatch." The other three had been in Liverpool before, and took delight in piloting me to places of interest, and in exhibiting to me as much of the wickedness and temptations of sailor life in Liverpool as I would consent to see or as they themselves were willing to encounter.

They were all decent young fellows, though, without much taste for coarse vices. They all hoped to be officers of ships some day, and had too much sense to impair their prospects by ruinous habits. And so, while we visited many of the concert halls, dance houses, shows, and other resorts where Jack was wont in those days to disport himself while in that port, our dissipations were of a mild and harmless sort, seldom going beyond a single glass of ale, a pipe or cigar, and an occasional joke with a pretty barmaid or waiter girl.

Captain Knight was an ardent apostle of temperance and used to deliver addresses at temperance meetings held in the vicinity of the docks for the special benefit of sailors. Such meetings were rather a novelty in Liverpool at that time, and a packet captain as a temperance lecturer was a curiosity. And so the meetings at which Captain Knight was invited to speak were considered by the ships' crews, as they expressed it, "as good as a show." The meetings were thronged accordingly by rough but, on the whole, orderly and respectful audiences, even if they were rather boisterous at times when an appropriate opening for applause relieved the strain of quietness and left them free to make a noise. The captain was a tactful man and knew sailors thoroughly and loved them, and, by force of a law as irresistible as gravitation, all decently disposed sailors loved him. As often as he saw that the effort to keep still and listen to his serious words was beginning to tell on the restless nerves of his auditors, he would let himself out with a humorous story or a burst of eloquence that gave them the opportunity to blow off their pent-up vitality in a round of vociferous applause.

One night, by special invitation of the captain, the four boys of the *New World*'s crew started out after supper to go to a meeting at which he was to speak. I had coaxed Jack to go along, although, he said, "I hain't no pertic'ler use for them temp'rance blowouts seein' as I've poured whiskey down my throat all my life an' 'spect to 'til I go ter Davy Jones."

On our way we met half a dozen of our crew swinging along the sidewalk and street singing in hilarious mood. We invited them to go along with us. Scenting some new form of dissipation in the wind, they fell in behind us and we reached the place of meeting where a noisy, jolly crowd had gathered. When we entered the hall, a piano and violin on the platform playing lively tunes helped the illusion that we had brought them to some new kind of music hall not frequented by them before. As they crowded into seats well up toward the front they began to call out for pipes and mugs of 'alf'n'alf and to curse the lazy barmaids who failed to put in an appearance.

Presently the music ceased and the chairman of the meeting, a dapper little old man with white hair dressed in half-nautical, half-clerical clothes after the manner of a Seamen's Bethel missionary, arose and, amid a confusion that completely drowned his voice, made a few introductory remarks that to the audience were a frantic pantomime of moving lips and waving arms, and introduced the speaker of the evening.

Thus Captain Knight, who had been sitting behind the piano, came forward to the front of the platform. As he began speaking in an easy graceful way, but in tones that were accustomed to battle with the noise of sea, wind, flapping canvas, and rattling blocks, the confusion gradually subsided. Our own men stretched their necks in bewildered amazement at first, and then as they took in the sturdy figure and genial face of their captain and found that their eyes were not deceiving them, they one after another ducked their heads and shrunk themselves into as small a space as possible.

"Wal I'm blowed if that ain't our Old Man," said one. "Wot the 'ells 'e doin' 'ere," said another. "Say, boy, wot sort o' show's this you've piloted us inter?" said a third. They began to hitch uneasily toward the end of the bench, and I thought for a minute that the whole crowd was going to bolt for the door, but the ring of the captain's voice, or some other subtle influence, seemed to hold them. The captain meanwhile had discovered us, and presently turning toward the musicians with a smile, signaled them to strike up a tune. Then he leaned forward over the edge of the platform and beckoned to me to come to him. I started up the aisle shaking in my shoes with the fear that he was going to give me a blowing up for bringing such a disorderly crowd into the meeting. My progress was followed by a chorus of catcalls, and suggestions to "cut and run youngster," "go overboard an' drown yersel'" and various other bits of advice of like character.

When I reached the front of the platform the captain bent over, and, in a kindly tone that at once scattered my fears, asked, "What shipmates have you got there with you, my boy?"

"Jack Corbett, Dick Brown, Tom Perkins and three or four more, Sir, besides the other boys."

"All right, you may go back to your seat."

Then he straightened himself up and assuming the tone and posture of command, shouted, "Main deck there, Jack Corbett."

Jack jumped to his feet as if a barrel of firecrackers had gone off under him and shouted back at the top of his voice, "Aye, aye, Sir."

"Come on the poop, Corbett, and lend a hand."

"Aye, ye, Sir," answered Jack, and he started up the aisle as promptly as if going to execute an order aboard ship. But he was very unsteady on his legs and lurched from side to side, fetching up against the end of a bench every now and then. He was followed by shouts of "Steady thar mate," "Now she rolls," and other encouraging remarks. Halfway up the aisle he stopped to steady himself against a bench, and was heard to murmur, "Wal she do roll dre'fal, an' no mistake. However we got up such a dev'lish sea in this 'ere channel's more'n I can on'stan', an' sh' mus' be a cranky ol' craft any how!" When he reached the steps leading up to the platform the captain and the chairman gave him a hand each and two or three sailors occupying front seats stepped forward and gave him a boost from behind with a friendly injunction to "Mind yer eyes and yer pins, matey," and so he was safely landed on the stage, looking very sheepish as to his countenance and shaky as to his legs and sort of doubled up amidships.

The captain led him to the middle of the stage, and after signaling the music to stop, put his hand on Jack's shoulder in a fatherly way, and turning to the audience said, "Now, my lads, this is Jack Corbett, one of the best all-round seamen I have ever known when he is rightly master of himself and I am proud to be the captain of the ship he belongs to and to call him shipmate. You see, men, the *New World* is a pretty big ship, but she isn't so long that friendly hands can't reach her length from quarterdeck to forecastle," and he turned and gave Jack a hearty handshake that, in his top-heavy condition, nearly capsized him.

The captain's compliments and familiarity flattered and pleased Jack immensely, and he tried to show his appreciation and pleasure by straightening himself up and saluting with much ceremony, which ended in a foolish grin and chuckle and a series of winks, that brought down the house.

"Now, Corbett, turn around and face the audience like a man, and let them see what sort of thing whiskey, when it gets the best of him, can make out of a first-class sailor man that never need hang his head before the Queen of England when he is sober."

Jack obeyed orders like the well-disciplined sailor he was, and faced the audience with an odd mixture of shamefacedness and attempted pride and dignity in his manner. The audience was in high glee, and no "turn" in a vanity show could have pleased them more. Greetings were showered on him from all sides.

"Unshackle yer jaw, Jack, an' give us a yarn."

"Taughten up on yer stan'in' riggin', matey, an' trim yer ballast a bit, an' let 'er go."

"Brace up yer figger an' swab that thar monkey grin offen yer face, an' make yersel' more like a parson if ye're goin' to preach." These were some of the greetings that were showered on him from all sides.

After giving them a few minutes for their fun without interfering, the captain raised his hand and the noise subsided. "Now, Corbett," he said in an undertone, "give them a piece of your mind."

Under the influence of the novel conditions, Jack had been gradually sobering up and pulling himself together. He was no fool and he knew it. He had a tongue in his head and knew how to use it on occasion, but he was more accustomed to holding forth pipe in mouth, seated on top of his chest in the forecastle or on a windlass head on the forecastle deck, than standing on the platform of a meeting ball. He stood a few minutes, shifting his quid from one cheek to the other, hitching up his trousers, and with his legs in the familiar position that sailors acquire in bracing themselves on an unsteady deck.

Then he said, "Now, mates, when them thar boys," pointing to us, "'ticed me inter this show, I hadn't no sech o' notion as I were goin' ter be stood up for a 'orrible 'xample, or as a horator 'long side o' Cap'n Knight, who knows more 'bout preachin' every day 'n the week 'n my clumsy 'ead could ever larn if I live 's long's that thar long-winded M'thursela feller. 'Tho' I makes no doubt the captain hi'self will allow as Jack Corbett knows more 'bout Rum an' Gin an' W'isky an' 'alf'n'alf an' all them bloomin' things as sets sailors' 'eads a buzzin' an' their legs a wobblin', 'n 'e'll ever larn. But I ain't no ways onwillin ter b'ere, an' ter be showed up, if it'll please the best skipper as ever stumped the weather side o' th' quarterdeck of a packet ship. An' that's wot Cap'n Knight is. An' I've sailed with a'most all of 'em, as many o' you fellers knows, 'specially them as hangs out a' Mike Walsh's boardin' house down Waterloo Deck way."

"Three cheers for Cap'n Knight," came from the *New World* benches, and they were given with a will by the whole house. When the enthusiasm subsided, Jack continued, "The cap'n's right about Jack Corbett. I ain't no landlubber, nor yet no kind o' slouch aboard ship, 'tho' I says it as maybe shouldn't. But the cap'n's said it afore me, an' I hain't no call to go agin 'im, seein' as 'e knows a sailor man w'en 'e sees 'im as well's any bloomin' skipper as navigates the stormy seas and sails the ocean blue."

Jack was dropping into poetry. "An' now mates, seein' as I hain't no ambition ter be no end of a horful 'xample, till my sails is closed up an' my anchor down in the last port wherever that may be, an seein' as by this time Jack Corbett's sense has got a top o' the rum as he'd loaded hi'self with afore he came in 'ere, I be just a goin' to put my tarry fist to the pledge this night, an' if any o' my shipmates or my ol' mates as I've cruised 'round with among the barrooms an' dance houses wants ter do the same, I ain't that selfish as I'd want ter m'nopolize the whole show. So I says, shipmates, come up an' ye'r welcome; come one come all, as we says w'en we stan's up afore the bar with our pockets full o' silver, an' our 'eads empty o' sense an' want to treat all the thirsty bums that's a-hangin' roun' with the'r thro'ts dry's the desert o' Sahary an' their mouths open wide's the main hatch."

Jack closed his speech with a salute to the audience and another to the captain, and then sat down on a chair which the missionary had brought forward in the meantime for his accommodation while the hall rang with such applause as only a room full of sailors can give.

It was customary at these meetings to accompany the serious business of exhorting to temperance with some form of entertainment adapted to nautical tastes. On this occasion, after a brief closing speech, the captain called out, "Boy Fred of the *New World*, come up and give us the Sailor's Hornpipe." The musicians started the tune, and Boy Fred, who was well known as an accomplished dancer, went forward and executed his task with grace and vigor, followed by some more exploits of voice and foot by other volunteer performers.

After the close of the meeting came the ceremony of signing the pledge. Jack kept his word and made his mark with promptness and decision. Several others followed with their marks or signatures, those who could write signing their names with more or less flourish and with evident pride.

I am sorry that I cannot record, as a part of this truthful narrative, that Jack kept his pledge to the end of his life. If I were writing a nautical romance, I should probably do so, as sailors have been known to keep temperance pledges. The best I can say in this case is that I never knew Jack to get drunk during the rest of our stay in Liverpool or on the voyage home. If the temptations of Cherry and Water Streets proved too much for him after he found himself once more in that sailor's paradise of which they form a part, it was only what has befallen thousands of others like him before and since.

On Sundays we usually went to church in the forenoon, in compliance with the captain's advice. In the afternoon we strolled about Liverpool, visiting the public gardens, looking at the fine buildings, and indulging in many boyish visions of some day becoming ourselves great merchants, ship owners or bankers. Sometimes we strayed out into the country where there were groves of trees, and picturesque lanes and pretty villas, and, even in this late autumnal season, many sweet sights and sounds of country life, with the busy city lying in the distance half-revealed under the veil of haze and smoke that seemed always spread over it. Occasionally we stopped at little wayside dairies and regaled ourselves with bread and cheese and milk. At other times we wandered along the docks, looking with curious interest at the strange craft from many lands, with their odd rigs, quaint models, and unpronounceable names, and listening to the queer speech and noting the fantastic attire of some of the crews, and inhaling the sweet odors of fruits, spices and gums, or the vile ones of hides and guano and oil, that gave hints of the different climes from which they had come. These were happy, careless days of freedom and of the unrestrained enjoyment of scenes and sights and sounds that were strange and full of interest.

There came an interruption to this daily round of work and play so far as I was concerned, when I was confined to my bed at the boarding house with an illness that lasted a week. The symptoms were sufficiently like those of cholera to cause no little anxiety and dread. Cholera at the time was prevalent in various parts of the world and was being spread to other parts in the ships that came and went. Captain Knight hearing of it from the other boys in explanation of my absence from the ship, came from his hotel to see me the same evening, and visited me every day until I was able to be about again. He gave orders for everything to be done that could be done for my comfort, and sent his own physician to see and prescribe for me. Knowing something of Jack's fondness for me, he asked me if I would like to have Jack come and stay with me and nurse me, and upon my nodding assent, feeling too ill and miserable just then to speak, he relieved Jack from duty aboard ship and sent him to me with orders not to leave me until I was well. The poor fellow was full of anxiety about me and his satisfaction at being assigned to this duty was beyond his power of expression in words, but was plainly read in the eagerness with which he sought to make himself useful, and his presence a pleasure to me. He proved, in spite of his rough manner, and his sometimes awkwardness in the performance of unaccustomed duties, a tender and assiduous nurse, his sincere devotion making up for any lack of experience or skill in the care of the sick.

As I appeared to grow worse for the first two or three days, the kind-hearted captain offered to send an experienced female hospital nurse to take care of me, but I shook my head, being quite content with Jack, and knowing full well that it would nigh break his heart to be superseded. The other boys and the mates, all of whom boarded in the same house, were also very kind and attentive, spending much of their time after the labors of the day were over in my room, except when Jack fearful of their tiring me would order them out.

"Now look a-here, you youngsters," he would say, "this ain't no fo'c's'le for spinnin' yarns in, nor yet no concert hall for c'rousin' an' jollyfyin', an' this 'ere boy ain't no haudience fer a v'ri'ty show, not wile Jack Corbett's 'sponsible fer 'im to the skipper, an' you boys has got ter be qui't wen yer in 'ere an' git out w'en I tells ye, or get yer 'eads punched." And the boys would file out, smiling and winking at me behind Jack's back. They were good fellows and we were all fond of each other, and they were not at all disposed to resent Jack's assumption of authority in my behalf.

To the mates he was, of course, more respectful, though not at all averse to letting them feel at times that he was in authority. "Now, Mr. Sargent, beggin' yer pardon, I reck'n e's 'ad all the talk as is good fer 'im this time, much as I knows 'e's fond o' hearin' your soothin' voice, but we've got ter pull 'im through this 'ere flurry an' 'e 'ain't got no 'ndurance yet—no more 'n a hinfant," and Mr. Sargent would get up and give me his hand with a good-natured smile and motion of his head toward Jack.

The landlord's wife was a buxom, motherly creature, red in the face from constant companionship with kitchen stove, wash tub, and ironing table, broad in the waist, bare in the arms most of the time, and soft in the heart. She would bustle in and out with offers of assistance and enquiries whether there was any-thing she could do for the "dear lad," in the brief intervals that she could snatch from her duties in cooking, washing and iron-ing for thirty or forty men and boys with appetites like bears, and whose occupation aboard ships, loading and unloading, overhauling and rigging, were not conducive to overmuch cleanliness.

And now I am going to record something that will doubtless excite the ridicule of any medical gentlemen who may chance to read it, and for which I can claim no other merit of justification than that it is literal truth. The landlord, a good-natured Scotchman, came to my room one day and said, "Naw, laddie, if ye're a min' to tak a bit dose that I'll put t'gither for ye, I'll war-rant 'twill make a new mon o' ye inside the naxt twainty-four hour, on the word o' Davy McBrian. It's wat I've stretened out the inside wuks o' mony a seafar'in' mon wi' in my time. It's chol'ry morbus ye've got an nae thing ither."

As I was getting desperate and the medicine I had been tak-ing seemed to be doing me no good, I agreed, after consulting with Jack, to take the "bit dose," a very irregular and disorderly thing for me to do without consulting the doctor, I can but own. In a few minutes the landlord brought his dose in a tin basin of about the capacity of an ordinary bread-and-milk bowl, which it nearly filled. With the natural impulse of a human animal before swallowing an unknown dish that is set before him, I first smelled it and then sipped a bit of it. It was very hot, and it smelled and tasted very strong of vinegar and salt and red pepper and mustard and other unsavory or fiery things, the prevailing impression being that of hot brim seasoned with bilge water, burnt gunpowder and live coals. After some hesitation, spurred on by the landlord's "Bolt 'er, laddie, 'ithout thinkin' o'er much wat ye're doin,'" and Jack's "Dowse yer, 'ead lights boy, an' let her go," I shut my eyes and swallowed the mess. For the next few minutes after it was down, I was in doubt whether the inside of me was a gun barrel just fired off or a steam boiler getting up steam. In an hour I was sleeping, as Jack told me afterwards, "like a month-old kid on 'is mother's breastworks," and in three days I was out for a walk with Jack. He had become so used to thinking of me, while ill, as "a hinfant," that he would have liked to trundle me about in a baby carriage or a perambulator if one could have been found big enough, and I would have consented. But as I was not ready to renew my infantile youth to that extent, I insisted on using my own legs and Jack had to be content with leading me by the hand when there was fear of losing me in a crowd or putting his arm around me over rough places.

In a couple of days more I was back at work aboard the ship and enjoying an affectionate welcome from all hands.

I have never had my doubt that the landlord's "bit dose" did the business for me. But as I have no medical diploma, and do not care to be handed up for prescribing without a license, I do not advise anyone to take it without consulting a doctor.

Chapter Seven ↜

We remained in Liverpool three weeks, and then, with a cargo of iron, silk, cotton and woolen goods, and general merchandise, and with a full cabin list, and three hundred and twenty emigrants engaged for the steerage, we hauled out of the dock and anchored in the river. The next morning at high tide our passengers and their luggage were brought off in river steamers and small boats. The anchor was again hove up, and with a fair wind and tide, we made sail to the royals and headed down the Mersey. At dark we had cleared the Skerries, and, bracing in the yards a point, with a good whole sail breeze a little abaft the beam, we were fairly started on our homeward voyage

For two or three days we had southerly winds and fair weather. Then the wind hauled to the northward and westward, and we had a succession of gales and squalls, with snow and rain and sleet. I soon realized that a sailor's life and work on the *New World* on the passage over was child's play in comparison with what it had now become, and now began to know something of the real hardships and perils of the sea.

There was in the *New World* none of the brutality of which so much is written in sea stories, and, alas, with too much truth, and which goes to make up so much of the hardship often suffered by poor Jack-tar—all the more exasperating because it was only and needlessly superadded to unavoidable hardships that are hard enough at best. My experience and observation throughout this and a subsequent voyage in the same ship convinced me that none was necessary.

We had, I suppose, about the average of packet ship crews, no better and no worse than others. But I never saw a blow struck by officer or man in that ship, nor belaying pin nor handspike used for any but its legitimate purpose, except once in quelling a mutiny among a lot of turbulent and riotous steerage passengers.

I have heard in the forecastle plenty of reminiscences of brutal treatment and of bloody fights between officers and men on board other packet ships. I have been shown scars of scalp, wounds that told of vicious blows from belaying pins or handspikes, other scars of knife cuts, and others where bullets from a captain's or mate's revolver were said to have gone in and come out. The same men who bore these marks and with the same dispositions and tempers, apparently, that they had carried into other ships, were there among the crew of the *New World*, and did not need to be knocked down, nor gashed, nor shot at, on board that ship.

What made the difference? The answer must be looked for on the quarterdeck. It is perhaps needless to say that the fountainhead of the character of a ship's personnel is in the captain. His disposition, his sentiments and his principles of action will diffuse themselves throughout the ship. His subordinate officers will take their cue from him, either spontaneously, or by compulsion. If he is brutal it is next to impossible for a mate to be decent and considerate toward the men, however kindly his disposition may be. If the captain is humane and reasonable and looks upon his crew as human beings to be treated accordingly, and is a man of firmness and decision, his officers, whatever their dispositions may be, or however tough their previous practices, will learn to keep their tongues and fists and belaying pins in check. The owners, too, will be induced to see that the provisions and stores are of good quality. To all these indications of a reasonable regard for their comfort and welfare, the crew will, ninety-nine times in a hundred, promptly respond.

And let it be thoroughly understood that the *New World* was not a philanthropic experiment put afloat for the purpose of demonstrating any humanitarian theory of reform in the government of ships' crews, nor a floating Sunday school. She was just a typical, practical packet ship of her time, out for business and to make money for her owners, and the ship was sailed and the crew was worked for all they were worth. She was fortunate in having a captain who knew the value of peace and contentment in the forecastle and of willing service on deck, who knew how to secure them, and whose disposition was in harmony with this knowledge.

Captain Ebenezer Knight after he left the packet ship service went, as I was informed, to San Francisco as agent of the Pacific Mail Steamship Co., where he died. What monument, if any, has been erected to his memory I do not know, but if this book shall ever be published, I want this page to be a tribute to his memory as a Christian gentleman, a thorough seaman, a kind and humane captain while at the same time a firm disciplinarian, and a sincere and fatherly friend to young men entering upon a nautical career under his command.

I have ever since felt a deep interest in the subject of the treatment of sailors. I have discussed it with officers and men. I have personally commanded many sailors on large yachts which I have owned and sailed. It is my conviction that most of the brutality on board ships, and of the conflict between officers and men, originates with the former and the quarterdeck, and not the forecastle.

The sailor is not naturally brutal. For the most part he is kind-hearted, submissive to authority, disposed to be peaceable when you will let him, and susceptible to decent treatment. It is only when he is goaded and bullied beyond endurance and exasperated by a sense of injustice, that the brute in him rises up and snaps at the other brute that is worrying him. Then that other brute, being clothed with authority, considers himself justified in bullying him some more and pounding him into submission and putting him in irons to punish the resentment that he has himself provoked. It is true that there are sometimes found among ships' crews murderous, mutinous rascals who must be subdued and kept in subjection by fear of the hand-spike and the pistol, but they are the exceptions, as every candid officer in the merchant service must admit.

These conclusions have not been reached in the seclusion of a ship's cabin or of a gentleman's library ashore. Nor have the observations on which they are based been made through the gold-rimmed eyeglasses of a philanthropic theorist. Actual life in the forecastle and a familiar knowledge of the sailor and his ways afford the warrant for their utterance.

Our work aboard the *New World* was now hard, unremitting and perilous. Hardly a watch passed without all hands being called, and a full watch below for anybody was rare. It was past the middle of December and approaching the severest part of winter in the North Atlantic. Alternations of snow and hail and rain freezing as it fell were almost constant. The rigging was much of the time coated with ice and several inches of snow on the deck were not uncommon. Reefs were put in and shaken out of the topsails sometimes several times a day, while topgallant sails and courses were furled and set almost as often. Squalls were frequent and vicious, and the ship was several times near her beam ends. The decks were deluged with heavy seas, and the idea of anything dry was, for many days at a time, only a memory of the past or a hope of the future. Our clothes were soaked, and with no chance to dry them, we went about the decks, or crept in and out of our bunks in the brief intervals below, wet to the skin. Frequently our wet clothes would be frozen stiff, and I have seen a pair of oilskin overalls, after a man had wriggled himself out of them, stand alone. The work on the topsail yards was especially severe. The shrouds and ratlines were often covered with ice, so that going aloft was difficult and dangerous. The foot ropes were also slippery with ice, and the reef points would freeze so stiff that we would have to twist them in our hands and break the ice off before we could knot them. We often had to take belaying pins aloft with us to knock the ice off the heads of the sails before we could gather them up for reefing or roll them up on the yards for furling.

Sometimes, when we had been leaning over a yard, working at reefing or furling a sail, with the rain and sleet driving in on us, we would find ourselves frozen fast to the yard.

During the trying period of which I have tried to convey some conception, Jack's care and solicitude for me were as sympathetic as they were invaluable. He seized every opportunity to thaw out and dry my clothes at the galley fire while his own remained wet and frozen. He took pains when we went aloft to furl or reef to get next to me on the yard and exhort me to be sure and grab onto him if I lost my hold or slipped at any time, assuring me that he would hold on for both of us. In trying to patch my only pair of boots he had seen that they were hopelessly gone to pieces, and one night I found at the foot of my bunk a pair of stout and serviceable shoes quite new that I had previously seen in the possession of a little Swede of about my size belonging to our watch. Thinking that they had got into my bunk by mistake, I took them to the man who told me they were no longer his, that Jack Corbett had bought them of him that morning for two pounds of tobacco and a flannel shirt. They fitted me very well, and as they were nowhere near being big enough for Jack's ample feet, I knew at once how they had found their way to my bunk. I could not suppress a choking sensation in my throat when I thought of the sacrifice Jack had made for my comfort, for I knew that he had no surplus of flannel shirts and that his stock of tobacco was running low. When I communicated with him, he reminded me that but for his advice about the whiskey, which had after all been of no use to me, having been so sadly wasted, I would have bought shoes instead, and closed the argument by saying, "It's no more'n square, boy."

One night we were out on the jib boom securing the head sails. There was a tremendous sea running, and at every plunge of the ship into it we were completely buried out of sight. When she rose again we would be carried high in air until we seemed to be on a level with the fore topgallant yard. While going up we worked at the sails and gaskets with all our might. Then as we felt ourselves plunging downward again and nearing the crest of the succeeding wave, the cry would be raised, "All hands hold fast!" With arms around the spar and our feet braced hard on the foot ropes, we would hold on for our lives while the sea swept over us until we emerged again drenched with water and glistening with specks of phosphorescent light. Jack was next to me, and at each plunge into the boiling sea I would feel his arm around my waist. How he managed to hold on with one hand and half support me with the other only a seasoned old salt could tell.

One terrible night, in which there seemed to be a peculiar concentration of all the elements of discomfort and danger that could gather around a ship in mid-ocean in winter, we had got down on deck after putting a close reef in the main topsail when the chief mate, looking up, saw a man still on the yard. The night was freezing cold. The air was full of hail and rain and sleet and driving spray. The wind was blowing a fierce gale, with furious squalls that seemed, sometimes, as if they would lift the ship bodily out of the water and blow her away to leeward like a feather. The ship, close-hauled, was driving into the teeth of the gale.

As every bit of available muscle was needed on the halyards, and at the sheets and braces, the mate shouted to the man to come down. As he made no movement even after the third mate's mighty voice had taken up the shout and repeated it several times, the officers were puzzled, and ordered two of us to go up there and see what the matter was. Jack and I went. We found the man nearly insensible, with his body and arms frozen to the yard, and his feet frozen to the foot ropes. To free him and get him down on deck was a difficult and dangerous task. After we had disengaged him by cutting away with our sheath knives the ice that held him fast, Jack supported him where he was, while I went into the maintop to look for some means of getting him out of his perilous position.

I was fortunate enough to find a coil of studding sail halyards and a tail block. Hanging the block around my neck, and taking an end of the halyards in my teeth, I climbed up to the topmast crosstrees, made the block fast, rove the halyards through it and carried the end down to the topsail yard and out on the yardarm to Jack. Leaving him to make it fast around our almost unconscious shipmate, I went back into the top and, when I got the word from Jack, hauled the line taut. Then, as Jack supported him cautiously along the yard, I took in the slack until we had him close in by the mast, when Jack called out: "Hold hard, boy." Taking a turn around a cleat, I held the man suspended until Jack joined me in the top, when, together, we carefully lowered away until he reached the half dozen pairs of ready arms stretched out to receive him.

To the reader who may have forgotten that the ship was not standing still, nor gliding leisurely over smooth water all this time, the foregoing may seem as easy and simple a performance as it is to describe it, but in that howling gale and tumbling sea, with the darkness of a stormy night over everything, it was no trifle. The cheer that came up from the deck and floated away on the gale gave token of what our shipmates thought of it.

Next day in the first dog watch, word came forward that the captain wanted the two men who had rescued a frozen shipmate from the main topsail yard the night before to come aft after supper. Jack and I went, with considerable honest pride swelling in our breasts. This was followed by much bashful quaking when, as we made our way aft, we saw that the captain had assembled the cabin passengers on the quarterdeck. The men of both watches had got wind that something out of the common was going on, and flocked after us. There we stood, Jack and I, with the captain and the cabin passengers in front of us, the officers a little to one side, our shipmates gathered behind, and a crowd of curious and wondering steerage passengers filling in the background.

The captain had been snatching a brief rest below when the incident of the night before occurred, and had known nothing of it at the time. He had heard of it in the morning, but no names had been mentioned.

The men of the sea are so accustomed to incidents that are thrilling and exciting at the time, to hair breadth escapes and perilous adventures following each other in quick succession, that the impressions they make are as fleeting and transitory as the changing forms of waves or clouds, each quickly losing itself in the one that follows. And so, after the brief excitement that had expended itself in the cheer that went up to Jack and me in the main top, little more had been thought of the incident that had called it forth.

As Jack and I stood before the captain, he turned to Jack and said, "What is your name, my man?"

"John Corbett, Sir" answered Jack, saluting in man-of-war fashion.

"Where is the other man?" asked the captain, looking around.

"This is him, sir," laying his hand proudly on my shoulder.

The captain looked surprised and incredulous.

"Do you mean to say, John Corbett, that you got that man down from the topsail yard, with nobody to help you but this youngster?" he asked.

"I mean to say, captain, beggin' yer honor's pardon, as him an' me done it, eq'al parts, share an' share alike. He done his part; no man in this 'ere ship could 'a done it better—beggin' all yer pardons, shipmates," and Jack saluted the crew with a backward wave of his hand. A murmur of applause from their direction signified that the apology was accepted.

It was the captain's turn now to look pleased and proud. He had a large bump of local pride and enthusiasm, this gallant captain, and hardy little Vermont with its green-clad mountains wooing the sky; its lakes and streams, homes of the pike and pickerel, the bass and the speckled trout; its fertile valleys and hillside farms; its sturdy men and handsome women and fleet horses; its maple sugar; its domestic and civic virtues; its love of liberty; and its heroic history, was the hub around which his emotions and memories revolved with a constancy that even the wide freedom of the sea had not diverted.

I found out afterwards from one of the cabin passengers who became confidential with me that the captain had been bragging a little at the cabin table a few days before about his Green Mountain boy, who coming aboard ship pale, and thin, and green, had shown so much pluck and endurance and aptitude for the sea.

He made us a neat little speech, and then shook hands with us, and introduced us to the cabin passengers, who all shook hands with us, and then he called on the crew to give three cheers, and ended up by ordering a "blowout" of fresh meat and vegetables from the cabin stores for dinner in the forecastle next day.

Chapter Eight ⁊

We had milder weather for a few days after this, for the most part cloudy and wet, but with intervals of sunshine in which we had opportunities for drying some of our wet clothes. Then gales and sleet and snow again, topped off with a hurricane, in which we lost four topsails in one day.

On that day, the ship was close hauled under close-reefed fore and main topsails, reefed foresail and main spencer. The sky was overcast and of a dull leaden hue everywhere, except for a sulfurous glow near the horizon to windward. Suddenly out of that quarter in the middle of the forenoon watch came a haze of rain and spray like a puff of smoke from a monster gun, accompanied with a roaring noise and a blow upon the staggering ship that might well have been compared to the concussion of a broadside. In a second, the fore topsail, with a succession of reports like musket shots, was flying in ribbons, with patches of it sailing away to leeward like white clouds against the leaden sky, or settling on the crests of the waves like exaggerated seagulls. A spare fore topsail was quickly sent aloft and bent. Just as they were sheeting it home, a fresh burst from the same quarter converted the main topsail into strips of torn canvas, streaming and flapping from the yard, or flying in bits on the gale.

I went with the men of our watch on the main topsail yard to unbend the torn fragments and bend a new sail.

This was my first experience with a torn sail, and I found it anything but holiday business, with the strips of heavy canvas some-times slapping our faces viciously, and sometimes winding them-selves around us as if to jerk us from the yard, and sometimes when we thought we had them well in hand, pulling themselves out of our grasp and beginning their mad career again.

After the sail was bent and while we were putting in the reefs, we heard again the sound which had now become familiar to our ears and, looking up from our work, we saw the new fore top-sail going the way of the others. An hour later the new main topsail was in shreds. By the time these were replaced, the worst of the hurricane was over.

A day or two later the wind had shifted to southeast, and, being now on the Banks of Newfoundland, we began to have a taste of foggy weather. Sometimes it was impossible to see one end of the ship from the other, and a man going aloft seemed to be climbing into the clouds by a ladder whose invisible top rested somewhere in the sky.

A big ship at sea in a dense fog is the theatre of many weird and ghostly effects. Sounds become exaggerated and distorted and the sense of their distance and locality becomes confused and contradictory. A voice shouting from aloft will sometimes seem as if it came from some distant vessel hidden in the fog, while ordinary conversation between men in the rigging will at other times come to the deck with a distinctness that suggests an invisible companion speaking at your side. Standing at the wheel, you seem to be steering a fragment of a ship into misty regions of nowhere. Aloft, you find yourself swinging in the air on a stick or rope without visible support, and with familiar voices and confused and mingled sounds reaching your ears that might be echoes out of space for all that you can see of their source. Out on the jib boom it is a queer sensation of riding on one end of a huge seesaw with the crest of a wave for a fulcrum and an invisible playmate at the other end.

On one of the foggiest of these foggy days, while, with half a gale of wind on the port quarter and under short sail, we were making nine or ten knots an hour, suddenly came a sharp cry from the lookout on the forecastle, "Breakers right ahead, Sir," and almost in the same breath from the mate, "Hard a port!" and then out of the fog ahead "Starboard there, lively," and, in an instant, there loomed up out of the mist the head sails of a large ship close hauled on the wind just across our bow. Then her foresail and foretopsail drew out past our headsails, all above her topsails being invisible. With a loud flapping of her canvas she came up into the wind in answer to her helm, and, as we fell off, we passed each other so close that our yards almost touched. As her stern swung across our bow and fell into a hollow of the sea, we were so near that, looking down from our topgallant forecastle, I could see the man at her wheel shifting his quid from cheek to cheek, as he recovered his helm to port, and cast an eye up at us. Her sails filled again, and before we had begun to realize the peril and escape, she shot out of sight into the fog, the rattling of her blocks and the voices of her men coming to us with strange and ghostly distinctness out of the invisible, as might those of a phantom ship.

During this stormy passage there was much unavoidable discomfort and suffering among the steerage passengers. Many of them had come aboard scantily furnished with warm clothing and with insufficient supplies of food. The price paid for steerage passage entitled the passengers to only a meager ration from the ship, prescribed by law to provide against actual famine and starvation. Beyond this, the steerage passengers were expected to supply their own food. A separate galley was provided for their use, where they did their cooking. As not more than a dozen or so could use the galley stove at one time, there was necessarily, among three or four hundred of them, much scrambling, hustling, pushing, and, sometimes, fighting for a chance.

Hungry stomachs paralyzed the gentler virtues for the most part and developed the brute instincts. That galley stove presented a daily object lesson on the supremacy of muscle, on the power of matter over mind in the human when the animal in him is dominant, and on the survival of the fittest. The feeble and the timid were crowded out by the aggressive and the strong. Unattended women with broods of hungry, clamoring children were shoved aside by brawny men who had nobody to care for but themselves. The women were left standing outside the galley with their pitiful little messes of oatmeal or barley or bacon, in rain and sleet, sometimes for hours. Unaccustomed as I was then to the sight of deprivation and hardship among the weak and defenseless, this wrought on my sympathies to such an extent that I could not stand it. I used often to take some shivering woman's dish from her hand and push and worm myself through the crowd of men to the galley stove and stand by it until the contents were cooked, and then fight my way out again to where the gaping mouths were waiting. My reward was usually a fervent "May the Lord bless you" or "the Blessed Virgin protect ye." Sometimes the children were told to wipe the porridge from their greedy little mouths and put up their smutty faces and "Kiss the kind sailor man."

The other boys were of the same mind, and we organized ourselves into a league for the aid and protection of helpless women and hungry children in the steerage galley. We used to have some lively scrimmages and lots of fun with the steerage bullies, and plenty of thanks from the women and feeble old men, and kisses from the babies. Boy Fred was the recognized leader in this chivalric warfare. He was strong and athletic, knew how to use his fists scientifically, and was a regular daredevil. Sometimes when his supremacy was disputed and his raids on the galley resisted by some bragging rustic who had won fistic honors on village greens or at county fairs, little matches would be quietly arranged to be fought at night under the gallant fore-castle, when the men of both watches and the passengers from the steerage would assemble to see fair play. Then bets of plugs of tobacco and of favorite pipes, and sometimes of flannel shirts and monkey jackets, would be recklessly offered and taken, and lost and won. These battles generally ended in the transfer of the stakes from the steerage to the forecastle, while the bloody noses and black eyes were mostly to be found in the former.

It was customary to turn all the steerage passengers out on deck at intervals to be aired, while their quarters were being cleaned and ventilated. It was hard on them sometimes in rough weather, but it was necessary in order to prevent disease, and for their own comfort and welfare in the end. None but those too sick to turn out were exempt from this ordeal. The ship's doctor would first go through the steerage and tack a card bearing his autograph to the front of each berth containing a passenger too sick or too infirm to be moved. All others must be turned out whether they liked it or not. Then a detail from the watch on deck would be sent below to clear the 'tween decks and fumigate while some of the male passengers were set to scrubbing and cleaning. The remainder, with the women and children, were compelled to stay on deck until the order was given to release them.

The boys usually had to take a hand in this business. It involved many conflicts between sympathy and duty. Feeble and seasick women whom the doctor had not ticketed as unable to go on deck would plead piteously to be allowed to stay below. Pale and ema-ciated children, who needed the air and light but whom loving but ignorant mothers shrunk from exposing to the wintry wind and storm, would be held up for our inspection with "Oh! dear sailor, can you have the heart to put this poor little thing out in the cold and wet?" The mother of God and all the saints would be entreated to forbid. Sometimes our sympathies would get the best of us. We would convince ourselves that the doctor had made a mistake and secretly connive at, or even plan ourselves, some cunningly contrived concealment. But with lazy men and healthy and robust women, we were obdurate. Despite their coaxing, often accompanied with attempted bribes unblushingly offered, on deck they must go. We were frequently obliged to drag them out of their berths by main force and carry them on deck kicking and screaming. In other cases, where force was likely to be too laborious or to involve too much inconvenience or delay, we would smoke them out with a red-hot shackle in a bucket of tar held in the berth until the smoke and fumes became intolerable. This never failed to subdue the most obstinate.

When the steerage was finally cleared, one of us would be stationed at each of the ladders leading down from the deck above. Armed with a handspike, we had strict orders to let no one come down. When a pair of legs would appear at the top of the ladder we would politely remonstrate. If the legs pulled themselves back again, well and good. If they continued to descend, we would remonstrate again in sharper tones. If this did not secure the desired result, a rap across the shins with the handspike would follow. That generally did the business.

It was during this stormy period that I first witnessed a burial at sea.

One day when the steerage passengers were thus gathered on deck for an airing, I noticed a discouraged looking woman in an attitude of listless dejection, holding a child between two and three years old across her lap. I recognized her as one whom I had sometimes assisted at the galley, and the little girl in her lap had often offered me her lips to kiss. She had been a bright gleeful little creature with blue wide-open eyes and yellow hair and red cheeks. On our few sunny days she had played about the deck, making friends with the sailors, sometimes peeping into the forecastle, or thrusting her curly head into the cook's galley, staring wonderingly at old Duffy at his work and admiring his shining black skin and bald brown head. She had evidently never seen a human specimen of his color before, and asked me once "'Oo painted him?" At another time, when she saw me with a pot of black paint and a brush, touching up the rail, she suggested that I should paint her "Jes' like mister cook."

Now as I passed once or twice where they sat, I noticed how still and white she was, and that her eyes were closed and her yellow curls looked limp and lifeless. Once I stopped, and asked the woman if the child was sick, and was told that she had been "ailin' several days." I stroked her cheek and lifted the curls from her forehead. They were damp with the mist and felt cold and clammy. The child did not stir. Stooping over her, I looked closer. The features had a strange set look, and the little mouth was pinched and drawn. I turned quickly away with a sinking at the heart, and brought the doctor. He felt the pulse, laid his hand lightly over the heart and looked startled. Then he gravely shook his head. The child was dead. She had died on her mother's lap, and the poor woman, worn with anxious watching through sleepless nights, had not known it. When she was told, there was no outbreak of grief. A careless observer might have thought she was indifferent and wanting in natural affection and sorrow, but I knew better. She was too much stunned to realize what had happened, too bewildered and paralyzed to know what she felt, or to give expression to it.

With the mother, silent and impassive, following me mechanically, I lifted the child tenderly in my arms, carried her down to the steerage, and laid her softly in their berth. I could not rid myself of the feeling that, unless I was very gentle, I should hurt her, so frail she seemed. Then the floodgates of a great grief were opened wide. The paralysis of feeling that had held them fast, gave way, and that dim steerage witnessed one of the most touching spectacles of human woe: a stricken woman weeping aloud by the side of her dead.

Next morning the order came to the sailmaker to prepare the little corpse for burial. I begged for Jack and myself the privilege of assisting him. He was a kind-hearted man, and I could not bear that ruder hands than his and ours should handle it, or that colder eyes be the last to look upon it. Some of the women of the steerage brought her to us dressed in her best clothes, after they had succeeded in persuading the mother that the parting time had come. We went into the sailmaker's room, taking one of the women with us, and shut and locked the door against intrusion by the curious.

We reverently laid the little form in its canvas coffin, already prepared, with the weights that were to sink it in a separate compartment at the foot, and carefully sewed it up. We were very tender about it, the feeling still possessing me, and evidently shared by the sailmaker and Jack, that we must not hurt her by so much as the least prick of a needle's point on the tiny folded hands, or a too harsh contact of the coarse canvas against the soft cheek. When all was finished we carried it out on deck. There have been statelier funerals, with pallbearers more numerous and of higher degree, but no princess was ever borne to the funeral altar by gentler hands or more reverent hearts than were at the service of this humble little waif of a packet ship's steerage.

The passengers and crew had already been assembled on deck, the main topsail was aback, and the ship's bell was tolling. A broad plank, with one end resting on the lee bulwarks just forward of the poop and the other on the shoulders of two of the boys, awaited its burden. The captain stood by with bared head and prayer book in hand, and the weeping mother sitting on a camp stool beside him. We laid the body on the plank. An impromptu choir from among the cabin passengers aided by rich voices from among the crew sang a hymn. The captain read in an impressive voice the beautiful Episcopal service for the burial of the dead at sea, and at the words, "We commit this body to the deep," the inboard end of the plank was raised, and the canvas coffin, with its contents, slid into the sea. I had climbed on the bulwarks to see the last of it. It had hardly touched the water before a breaking wave, with its swirl of foam, hid it from sight. The thought of it sinking into unexplored depths haunted me for days. Whether it had become the prey of sharks, or found its way to some secluded coral grotto or marine bower, there to be watched over and guarded by the kindly fairies and brownies of the deep, until the sea should give up its dead, who could tell?

"The Lord gave and the Lord hath taken away; blessed be the name of the Lord," came in deep and solemn tones from the captain. "Amen," responded many earnest voices. Then the yards were trimmed in, the sails filled, and the ship, bending to the strong breeze, fell off to her course. The decks resumed their everyday appearance, and, except in the heart of the sorrowing mother, and in mine perhaps, the impression of what had passed was as transient almost as the ripple caused by the plunge of that frail little body into the sea.

We had three more deaths before reaching port. I have since seen many burials at sea, but none ever impressed me like this first one.

Chapter Nine ✧

Five days later, while on the lookout forward at night in the middle watch, I saw, as the ship rose on the crest of a wave, what looked like two parallel stars close to the horizon. The night was overcast and stormy, and no stars were elsewhere visible in all the sky. I wondered if there was a rift in the clouds out there to windward through which these had glimmered. As we sank in the trough of the sea, they disappeared. As we mounted the next wave I saw them again, and pointed them out to the man on the lookout with me. Leaning forward, he gazed intently for an instant, and then, turning his face aft and making a speaking trumpet of his hands, he shouted, "Highland Lights on the weather bow, Sir!"

Again, as when I had seen them last, they seemed like a pair of friendly eyes, now watching for our return as then they had followed us out to sea.

The wind had been blowing from the northwest since the morning before, with gathering signs of a repetition of the experiences of the earlier days of the passage. Before daylight it had freshened to a gale, with snow and sleet and freezing rain, and Sandy Hook dead to windward twenty miles away. For three days we were beating about, with the Highlands in sight most of the time, making but little headway, and, a part of the time, hove-to and drifting to leeward. Toward evening of the third day we made the lightship and glided in past the Hook, covered with ice and with half a foot of snow on the deck. Shortly after dark we came to anchor in the lower bay.

Next morning we were taken in tow, and, after a couple of hours' detention at quarantine while our passengers were inspected by the doctors, we proceeded up the East River, and, before dark, were fast to the wharf at the berth we had left two months and ten days before.

The moment the ship touched the wharf, most of the crew, after the fashion of packet sailors in those days, considering the round voyage for which they had shipped at an end, sprang ashore and surrendered themselves, the willing prey of the boarding house runners who swarmed around them—an ill-favored, cursing, foul-mouthed, rascally lot—Jack's worst enemies in the guise of friends. In a few minutes they were crowding the nearest saloons and filling themselves with bad whiskey, to which they were ostensibly being treated by the runners, but which, in fact, was going to swell the bills on the strength of which their month's advance when they shipped again would be confiscated.

The boys, with two or three of the steadier men, stayed by the ship and helped the officers in putting things to rights. We slept aboard that night and next morning, with my bag on my shoulder, I walked up to Cortland Street Ferry and crossed the Hudson River to Jersey City. I astonished some relatives living there who had last seen me pale and thin in broadcloth clothes, kid gloves and patent leather boots, by walking in on them in my rough sea clothes, with brown cheeks, tarry hands, and a gait that seemed to suggest that their house was rolling and pitching in a seaway.

The youngest child of the family, a little girl three years old, on catching sight of me evidently connected me with that mysterious being usually painted in the imagination of little children in very dark colors, who is always coming to carry them off to same dreadful place if they are not good. Running behind her mother, she clung convulsively to her skirts and began to cry. Before half an hour had passed, however, she became convinced that I was not the "brackman" at all, but her "tuzzen weally and twuly," and was sitting contentedly on my knee exploring my pockets for peanuts and candy. By bedtime she had preempted my lap for a cradle. Subsequently this became so much a subject of contention between herself and her next older sister, aged five, that I had to establish a system of "watch and watch" and rock them to sleep alternately. They used to call it their "thip," and begged me to make the waves big by rocking as hard as I could.

That night, every time I fell into a doze, the room in which I slept was converted into a forecastle and, as the wintry wind whistled and roared around the house, and a loose blind slammed here and there, I expected every minute to hear all hands called to shorten sail. And when one of the older children pounded on my door in the morning, I shouted "Aye, aye," and jumped out of bed with a noise that sent her flying downstairs in dismay, with some sort of idea that her big cousin had gone mad with the hardships of the sea, of which he had been telling at the supper table.

That morning I visited the ship, received the balance of my pay, recovered my gold watch and shore trunk, and bade the officers and boys goodbye; not without regretful emotions, for my life among them, though rough, had been pleasant and genial, and brightened by many kindly acts.

A few days after, as I was going to Brooklyn with a young lady, having resumed my shore clothes and covered my mahogany colored hands with a pair of new kid gloves and my head with a tall hat, I ran up against Jack, just as we were about to cross South Street to Fulton Ferry. He did not recognize me in that rig until I called him by name, when he overwhelmed me with expressions of joy at meeting me again, for, as he explained, he thought he had lost me forever.

The young lady looked on and listened with amused astonishment, the forcible manner in which Jack, just mellow with whiskey, gave vent to his feelings, being quite new to her. Presently he asked me to take a drink with him in the saloon on the corner, "Jes one" he pleaded "with an old shipmate." I tried to explain to him, half in whispers and half in pantomime, that it was impossible. "Don't you see, Jack, that I have a young lady with me," I remonstrated, shaking my head and pointing my thumb over my shoulder.

"Never mind, boy, bring the gal along too," roared out Jack and then turning toward her and saluting in his best man-of-war style, "Beggin' your pardon, miss, but you won't mind takin' a drink with yer sweetheart's old shipmate?"

This was too much for the young lady, and she darted across the street toward the ferry entrance, convulsed with mixed sensations of amusement and fright, and hardly knowing whether she ought to laugh or cry or be angry. I finally coaxed Jack to let me off for that time, assuring him of my undying affection, and, crossing the street, rejoined her. As we passed into the ferry entrance, I turned and waved my hand to Jack. He saluted in return with an extra flourish, and swinging his cap in the air, called on the bystanders to give three cheers.

And that was the last I saw of Jack for thirty years.

Chapter Ten ✌

I t is but fair to explain, in defense of myself against the suspicion that this was due to neglect or indifference on my part toward my faithful chum. I did not forget my old shipmate and friend. I frequently sought him among the sailor boarding houses, saloons, and shipping offices, and along South Street after our parting.

I frequently visited the old boarding house in Water Street where I had first fallen in with him. I called on Ben's widow and her daughter in Brooklyn, and found that he had been there shortly after the return from our voyage in the *New World*, loaded as usual with things for their comfort and cheering them with his rough and ready sympathy and encouragement, but they had not seen him since. They remembered me, and the little girl, still more wan and emaciated than when I saw her before, asked me to come to her and putting up her arms as I had seen her do to Jack, kissed me softly on the cheek. "For dear Jack's sake," she said.

I went to the Seamen's Savings Bank and found that he had drawn his money a week after our parting, having been accompanied and identified by the keeper of a well-known sailor boarding house with a bad reputation for shanghaiing and robbing his patrons. During a second voyage in the *New World*, six months after my return from the first, I inquired of the officers, who all remembered him, and of my new shipmates, several of whom had known him, but none of them had seen or heard of him since the previous voyage. I inquired about the docks and sailor boarding houses in Liverpool with a like result.

Upon my return from this second voyage, I called again at the place in Brooklyn where Ben's widow had lived, and learned from the neighbors to my great sorrow that the little girl had died and her mother had gone away to friends in Maine. Failing to find him or hear from him, I was forced to the conclusion that he had been shipped off to sea while not in the full possession of his faculties and under another name, as so many sailors disappear from sight leaving no record behind.

For two or three years afterwards, I never found myself in the neighborhood of South Street, and of the wharves and ships without thinking of him, and looking about me in the hope of running across him. Finally, the expectation of ever seeing him again faded out of mind, and he became interwoven with the ship and the sea, the officers and the boys, sunshine and storms, and all the rest of it, into a sort of composite memory picture of my brief but exciting career as a sailor on this and the subsequent voyage.

PART SECOND
Ashore

Chapter Eleven ✣

I was sitting in my private office one day, busy with corre-spondence, when word was brought me that a man outside wanted to see me. "He is a rough-looking old fellow, something like a sailor, and I thought he might belong to your yacht, or be someone who you are interested in," explained the clerk in apol-ogy for disturbing me. There were so many "rough-looking" people in whom I was interested in those days, that it was well understood in the office that I was not to be denied anyone because he did not look like a bank president or a capitalist.

"Tell him to wait a few minutes," I said. When I had finished the letter I was dictating, I went out to see who my rough-look-ing visitor might be.

I found him hat in hand, withdrawn into a corner of the outer office, with an air of getting himself into as small a space as pos-sible lest he might be in somebody's way.

"Well, my man, did you want to see me?" I asked, holding out my hand.

"I wanted to see Mr. Hatch, Sir, if I might be so bold," he replied, looking abashed.

I had grown into rather a portly middle-aged gentleman with a bald head and side whiskers sprinkled with grey, and with the air of a prosperous man of family and business. I was as unlike in appearance to the slip of a youngster I had been thirty years before as well could be. "I'm Mr. Hatch," I said.

The man's countenance fell and he looked greatly disappointed. "I'm afeared 'tis all a mistake, Sir. Ye can't be the gent as I were lookin' fer, and I hope y' won't think hard o' me for disturbin' yer honor," he said, and began to move away toward the door.

His manner interested me. I had a warm place in my heart for old sailors and for the sort of character he seemed to be, and never lost an opportunity to draw them out.

"Perhaps there's no mistake after all," I said, smiling encouragingly. "Tell me what you wanted with the gentleman you were looking for, and it may be I can help you out."

I thought he might be wanting to get into Sailors' Snug Harbor, where I had helped a number of ancient mariners to anchor, or that he might be looking for a chance on a yacht, though he looked rather old for that.

My friendly and familiar manner emboldened him. A look half of enquiry and half of hope gleamed in his eye, and shifting his weight from one leg to the other, he looked in my face with a curious mixture of boldness and bashfulness, and said, "Did ye ever happen to know a man o' your name, beggin' yer honor's pardon, as went to sea in the packet ship *New World* from New York ter Liverpool about th' year forty-nine?" he asked. "He were a gentleman's son, an' I'm bound to say, a gentleman hi'-self, though he did live in the fo'c'sle and do sailor work and never put on no airs. Maybe he might be a son o' yourn," he put in suddenly, as if a new thought had struck him.

The thought of myself as my own father thirty years before made me laugh. "I went to sea in the *New World* in forty-nine myself," I said. His face fairly shone now.

"Maybe ye don't happen to remember yer old chum, Jack Corbett, as was shipmates wi' ye an' used to mend yer clothes and teach ye how to do things aboard ship, beggin' pardon agin," and he saluted with his right hand to his forehead and a scrape of his left foot to the rear.

"Yes, I remember Jack Corbett very well. Do you know what has become of him?" I asked.

"It's 'im as is standin' right afore your honor this minit," and he saluted again.

I had become rather suspicious of pretended old shipmates, having had a dozen or more battered old tars claiming that relationship since I had risen in the world, and of whom I could not awaken the slightest recollection, or whose identity did not bear the test of enquiry as to dates, particulars etc.

One in particular, then in Sailors' Snug Harbor, had been to me only a few months previously representing himself as an old shipmate of mine. He told me that, moved by grateful remembrance of kindnesses I had shown him, he was making a full-rigged model of the *New World* as a present for me. He said he had the hull and spars all finished, and it only remained to rig her and make the sails. The linen for the sails and cordage for the rigging, together with miniature blocks, belaying pins, steering wheel, anchors, etc, to make all complete would cost about five dollars. If I would let him have that amount, he could have the ship all ready for me as a Christmas present, while if he waited to get his next pension money he was expecting from another source, it might delay the work so as to deprive him of the pleasure of getting it finished in the time on which his heart seemed very much set. I had let him have the five dollars, and had never seen him since—nor the ship. The place on top of a bookcase in my library where I had intended to put it has remained vacant to this day. I meant to be very sure of my man this time before giving him the confidence due between old shipmates.

I had very distinct recollections of my experiences on the *New World* which had been kept alive by occasional narratives of the more interesting incidents for the entertainment of family and friends. I remembered Jack and the part he had borne in my nautical training, but the lapse of thirty years is apt to dim the memory of faces, as well as to work many changes in them.

"If you are Jack Corbett and were with me in the *New World*, tell me something that happened on the voyage." I said. "What time of the year was it?"

"We sailed nigh the beginnin' o' November, Sir, and come back last half o' January."

This was correct, and my faith began to rise, but it might be only a shrewd or lucky guess.

"Whose watch were we in?" I asked. As I had been in both watches on my first voyage, this question might trip a guesser.

"Second mate's watch first off, first mate's watch after, you an' me," he answered promptly.

True again, and I thought I began to see something familiar in the eager, weather-beaten face before me. Certainly if this was Jack, he had an excellent memory; if not, he was a good guesser.

"Tell me something else out of your own head, without my asking questions," I said.

By this time, he had drawn nearer to me and had lost much of his bashful manner. A shrewd smile gathered around his mouth and there was a twinkle in his eye. Leaning forward, he put his lips close to my ear, with one hand shielding our faces, and said in what he intended for a confidential whisper, but was in fact a kind of hoarse chuckle that might have been heard in a gale of wind.

"I say, boy, d' ye call to mind about the jug o' whiskey? And the sov'rin I made a hobble of?" The chuckle grew more subdued, with a breath of awe in it, but more triumphant, "And the ghost, boy; sure you mind the ghost."

I did "mind the ghost" as well as the jug of whiskey and the sovereign, and my doubts vanished. I grasped his hand again, and with a hearty, "Bless my soul, old shipmate, I'm glad to see you." Our relations of thirty years before seemed to merge naturally into the present.

Jack had drawn back a little, evidently somewhat shocked at his sudden burst of familiarity and disturbed by misgivings as to how it would be received, and resumed his deferential air. I invited him into my private office, and making him take a seat in a cushioned armchair, which he sank into with some hesitation, and offering him a cigar, I soon had him at his ease. I asked him to tell me about himself, since we had last met.

"Y' see," and he hesitated a second. "Y' see, cap'n"—he evidently realized, as he looked at my substantial figure and bald head, the incongruity of the old familiar "boy," and felt at the same time that "sir" and "your honor" were too formal and distant. "A few days after I parted from you, I got shanghaied an' shipped off in a bark bound for the Medit'ranean. I'd been on a spree for a week an' lost my head altogether. Everybody was headin' for Californy then, y' know, to dig gold, an' sailors was a crowdin' into them clippers an' 'twas hard to pick up crews for any other part o' the world; an' when they couldn't get 'em fair an' aboveboard, they got 'em foul. That bark were a rotten old tub an' nigh drownded us all goin' over. She was condemned an' sold by the agents at Naples, an' we was paid off an' discharged.

"I come back to New York on a fruiter; an' then I catched the Californy fever m'self an' shipped aboard a big clipper called the *Sov'rin of the Seas*, loaded with all sorts o' truck, all the way from full-rigged houses stowed away in pieces in the hold, to spades an' shovels an' pitchforks an' hairpins, with a sprinklin' o' babies cradles an' fryin' pans. We had a lot o' passengers, swells in the cabin an' countrymen an' toughs 'atween decks, all bound for the gold diggin's an' every mother's son of 'em expectin' to come home loaded with gold inside a year. They used to lay awake o' nights contrivin' the best kind o' ways o' gittin' it home safe, an' a plannin' how as they'd spend it. Some of 'em had the farms, or the mansions on Fifth Avenoo, or the country seats, they was goin' to buy all picked out aforehand, not to mention sich trifles as the hosses an' kerridges an' yachts an' other fixin's, jes' to work off the surplus as they didn't know wot else to do with it. Most of the chaps from around the docks in New York was a plannin' for saloons on the Bowery, 'reg'lar gilded palluses' they called 'm with marble barrooms in front an' lookin' glasses, an' shootin' gall'ries down cellar, an' gamblin' rooms upstairs, an' cockpits an' boxin' rings out in th' back yard.

"They was all in sich a hurry to git there and git to shovelin' gold, you'd a thought their skins wouldn't hold 'em. The captain an' officers, they was in a hurry too, 'cause there was big money in them trips an' the owners offered extra pay for quick voyages out an' back, so 'twas drivin' her, an' drivin' her, all the time, night an' day, an' no rest for poor Jack. 'Twas s'ls out an' s'ls in, an' royals an' skys'ls set an' furled, a dozen times a day, an' the ship under water an' everythin' flooded 'alf the time.

"All this talk about the gold that was to be had for the pickin' of it up kind o' set me wild. When we got to San Francisco, I deserted the ship with most of the rest of the crew, an' started for the gold diggin's, me an' my chum, Dick Brown, goin' in company. We didn't get much of any gold, but Dick got a bullet in 'is heart from a drunken blackguard of a miner, an' I thought I had got enough o' gold diggin', an' made my way back to San Francisco alone, a'most starved to death, 'ithout enough clothes on my back or flesh on my bones to sarve for a two-year old baby or a livin' skeleton in a museum.

"Then I shipped on another clipper back to New York. Sich a lot o' crews had deserted an' gone a-gold huntin', sailors was scarce, an' big wages was offered for the home'ard bound passage. After that I sailed in different ships to almost every port in the world. In 1862, bein' in New York again, I 'listed in the Navy an' sarved all through the war. I got this aboard th' *Hartford* at Mobile from a piece o' shell as bursted nigh the gun I was sarvin 'at, an' killed three o' the gun's crew an' wounded all the rest but one." Pulling up the right leg of his trousers, he showed me a long ragged-looking scar diagonally across the calf.

"After the war, I tuk to the clippers agin an' made more voyages to San Francisco an' some in tea ships to Chiny an' Japan. Then I got tired o' long voyages, an' kind o' hankerin' for th' old country an' for old times an' went to shippin' aboard Liverpool packets agin, but they warn't wot they was when you an' me was in the *New World*. The steamers was a crowdin' of 'em out an' takin' all the passengers

"They didn't keep the packets up in the same style as they used ter. Smaller crews an' poor grub an' hard work made it a dog's life aboard of 'em. I went two or three voyages in the *New World* an' was in her the last voyage just afore she was laid up. An' when I was aboard that old ship, I couldn't keep my mind off o' thinkin' o' you, nor my heart from a pinin' for ye. Many's th' time I was layin' in the same bunk in the port fo'c'sle, where I used to be an' you in yourn over me sleepin' like a hinfant—you mind which them bunks was I don't doubt—an' sometimes when I'd wake up sudden, I'd put my hand up an' feel whether or no you was there, an' when I'd find nobody in the bunk (for we was short-handed an' 'twas empty) 'twould gi' me a turn, until I'd get broad awake enough to remember as how 'twarn't the old voyage I was a sailin' but another. I use' ter wonder wot had become o' you. Sometimes I thought maybe as ye'd stuck t' th' sea an' growed to be captain, an' every new ship I'd go aboard of, I'd look to see ye like as not on the quarterdeck.

"Another time I'd think as ye'd got to be a rich swell, an' forgot all about poor Jack, an' agin' I'd mourn ye as dead an' gone. Every time I was in this port, I'd try to find somebody as knowed ye. An' when I'd run across them as was shipmates with us in the *New World*, I'd ask 'em if maybe they'd ever happened to sight ye or hear o' y'r bein' reported anywhere. But I couldn't get no tidin's o' ye whatsomever until yist'rday, I met Mr. Sargent as used to be third mate o' the *New World*—you remember Mr. Sargent—he's a stevedorin' now for Grinnell, Minturn & Co., as used to own the Swallertail Line which the *New World* was one of. 'E told me as how you was a great banker up here, but warn't a bit of a swell, an' was jes' like you used to be when you was a boy aboard ship, an' 'ow you'd helped 'im to get a place for 'is boy, an' you was allus glad to see an old shipmate, an' didn't make no difference whether he were on the quarterdeck or in the fo'c'sle. I come up here yist'rday an' when I took in wot kind o' place it was, I was a-feared to come in, an' just hung 'round the door outside, thinkin' as maybe I might sight ye goin' in or comin' out. Y' might ha' passed me that way a dozen times an' I not knowed you from the Prince o' Wales. You see, I couldn't git ye out o' my mind as the slip of a lad I knowed in the *New World*; an' Lord, who'd ever a thought o' you bein' him.

"I thought it all over last night, an' says I to m'self, 'Jack Corbett you're a chicken-hearted old fool; that there boy as you was chums with in the *New World* ain't a goin' to give ye the cold side o' 'is gizzard, not if he was the Emperor o' Rooshy'. An' so today, I made bold to come in."

"I am glad to see you, and glad you did come in, Jack." Then I told him how, after our parting at Fulton Ferry thirty years before, I had looked for him high and low among the saloons and boarding houses and along the docks; how I went to the savings bank and found he had been there and drawn out his money in rather suspicious company, and feared he had been robbed; how I had called twice at the widow's in Brooklyn, and the second time found that the little girl was dead and the mother had gone away. I told him about my second voyage in the *New World* and my enquiries for him among the officers and crew and among the boarding houses and sailor's resorts in Liverpool.

All this evidence of my interest in him pleased him immensely, and as he said, made him "proud."

"Yer were right about the bank, Cap'n. W'en they shanghaied me they got every dollar o' w'at ye'd 'elped me to stow away, an' sent me off dead broke, an' nary a decent rag to my back."

Then I asked him about the widow and the little girl, and whether he knew what became of the mother after the little one died.

"Well, ye see, I was there th' next week after you an' me parted. W'en I come back fr'm that thar voyage to the Medit'ranean I were tellin' ye of, I went there, an' 'twere then the little gal had died the day afore. I 'elped the mother to bury her in th' big graveyard over there as they called Greenwood, an' put a bit o' stone over 'er in honor o' Ben, an' 'is name along o' 'ers cut into it. Then the mother went away to 'er folks in Maine, as the neighbors told ye, 'cause wi' Ben an' the little gal gone, she 'ad no call to stay by 'erself. I didn't set eyes on 'er agin fer nigh on two year. That was after I come back from Californy, an' happenin' to go in a coaster to Maine. Fer want o' anything better jes' then, I got leave from her w'en she were unloadin' in Portland, an' went to the town the widow had gi'n me the name of about twenty mile away.

"I found 'er livin' in a house as looked so fine I were almost 'shamed to go in. But I made bold, an' she gi' me a welcome 's if I'd ben an admiral. Ye see she'd got married to a feller w't had the biggest store in the place an' a big lumber camp up in th' woods an' a span o' fast 'osses, an' was kind o' boss o' the town. W'en 'e come t'ome an' she interdooced me to 'im, 'e didn't put on no more airs 'an Ben would, an' said he knowed all about me, an' called me shipmate one minit an' Mister Corbett the next. They made me stay to supper an' then they wouldn't take no fer 'n answer but I must stop aboard all night. 'E offered to gi' me a job in 'is store if I'd stop altogether, but I warn't ready to leave off sea-goin' then an' take to no land-lubber jobs, an' so I told 'im I were much obliged an' to think no 'arm o' my refusin', an' bid 'em good-bye an' went back ter th' old dog's life.

"I went to see 'em once or twice after that w'en my travelin' tuk me that way an' I had some letters from 'em as I couldn't read 'cept some shipmate 'elped me out. Ye know, cap'n, sailors wanderin' 'round the arth ain't much on that kind o' thing, an' I haven't heard nought about 'em now for nigh on twenty year, an' more'n likely they be dead or think old Jack's gone ter Davy Jones, whar maybe 'e orter be afore now. But I tell ye, it soft me up th' way them two used me, jest a rovin' good-fer-nothin' son-of-a-gun; an' many's the time a-thinkin' about it, I've belayed doin' some'at as might make 'em an' the little gal 'shamed o' me if they knowed about it."

I asked him how long he had been ashore this time, and when he was going to sea again, and where bound.

"Well, ye see cap'n, that's jes' war 'tis. I don't want t' go t' sea no more," Jack said. "I'm a-gittin' old an' stiff, an' ain't no good aboard ship alongside o' them young fellers as is fillin' up the ships an' a crowdin' out the old hulks like me. An', then agin, sailin' ain't wot it used to be anymore. Them steamers has took the life out of it. I went in 'em two or three voyages but I couldn't git wonted to 'em wit' th'er blowin' an' whistlin' an' hissin', an' expectin' they was goin' ter blow up every minit. A sailor don't mind bein' drowned fair an' square when his time comes, 'cause it's his natural death, but t' be blowed up, or scalded t' death, or b'iled, ain't no way fer him to part company with hi'self.

"I been shipwrecked thirteen times an' 'though I can't swim no more'n a puppy with a stone 'round his neck, I got off every time. I've 'bout concluded I ain't meant fer Davy Jones' locker nohow an' maybe the Lord's planned it for my old bones t' be laid up somewhere in a shore burying' ground. That's one thing as I wanted to see you about, thinking' as maybe you might 'elp me to some sort o' landlubber's job."

Here Jack's voice sank to a confidential tone that was almost a whisper as he leaned toward me and said in a kind of shame-faced way, "Ye see, two or three voyages ago, I went an' got myself spliced. Her name's Clementina. We ain't no great on spoonin' but Clementina she thinks as how she'd like to set her eyes on me oft'ner 'n once or twice a year. I can't deny I feels the same consarnin' her."

While listening to his narrative, tender reminiscences of his kind and constant care for me in the old days at sea made my heart soft toward him and my eyes moist. I determined that the remainder of his life should be as smooth and peaceful as I could make it.

"You are quite right, Jack," I said. "I wouldn't go to sea any more if I were you under the circumstances. Of course you must stop ashore, or close by, and look after Clementina. We'll see what can be done."

"Beggin' yer pardon, cap'n, but it's Clementina as looks after me when I'm ashore," said Jack, looking over his shoulder in a deprecatory way, as if apologizing to Clementina for me, for supposing that she needed Jack to look after her.

"How would you like to go in a yacht, just cruising around the coast and home every few days?" I asked.

"I ain't no ways spry enough nor smart-lookin' enough to go in them sportin' craft. They ain't no place for a ol' shellback like me," he said, half in contempt for "them toy things," as he used to call them, and half in deprecation of his own growing infirmities.

"What do you say to Sailors' Snug Harbor then?" I asked.

"I ain't so far gone as that yet," he said, straightening himself up. "I'm able to earn my livin' I reckon for a few more years, an' 'til I can't do that no longer, I don't want t' be dismantled an' laid up like an old hulk t' rot, an' Clementina'd never hear to 't."

"Well, Jack, I have been thinking out something that perhaps will suit you and Clementina, and fit all around," I said. "I am living down the bay right alongside the water, and have got boats and fishing tackle and about a dozen children—just eleven all told by actual count—five boys and six girls. They are all fond of the water and are either paddling around on top of it in the boats, or fishing, or swimming, or wading up to their necks in it, most of the time. They need somebody to watch them and keep them from getting drowned, and to take care of their boats and their fishing things and keep the boathouse in order. Now, how would you like to come out there and live with us, and be boatswain of the place and the captain of the pier and the boat landing, and look after my young sailors, and lend a hand with the gardener now and then, and help with the pigs and chickens?"

While I was making this proposal, Jack's countenance was a study. It was clear that he was in doubt how to take it. Pleasure at the alluring prospect, doubt as to whether his ears were deceiving him, with occasional shadows of pain, as the suspicion that perhaps I was trifling with him came into his mind, chased each other in succession across his rugged but expressive face.

"Is it makin' a fool of ould Jack ye be?" he said at last, and a couple of big tears stole out of his eyes and rolled down his cheeks. The doubt and the pain had undoubtedly got the upper hand for a moment. Jack's peculiarities of speech became more pronounced, and the Irish brogue, mixing with the cockney dialect he had picked up in English ships and about the Liverpool and London docks, which was at other times less noticeable, asserted itself more distinctly when he was deeply moved. The cockney features of his dialect were intermittent. Sometimes he would drop his h's all about in a most promiscuous and reckless way and pick them up again and tack them on where they were not at all needed; while at other times—in the same sentence perhaps—he would keep them where they belonged.

All this gave to his speech a curiously mixed and variegated character, rich and entertaining to the ear, but exceedingly difficult of uniform expression in print. We soon found out that with his advancing years Jack's heart had grown soft, and tears came to his eyes as readily as to those of a child. It was interesting to notice the contrast between his rough exterior and the tenderness of heart that betrayed itself when his feelings were touched.

"Not a bit of it, Jack, I am in dead earnest—never was more in earnest in my life," I answered. "What do you say, will you ship with me and take that berth?"

"If I didn't, my name wouldn't be Jack Corbett," he answered, his face brightening. "I'm ready to sign th' articles this minute."

"Never mind the articles, Jack, I am not afraid you will desert the ship, but to show you I mean business, here is your month's advance," and I handed him some money. This appeal to the custom of binding bargains between ships and sailors was convincing, and the last cloud vanished from Jack's face.

Not to be outdone by me in the exhibition of confidence, Jack declined to take the money, remarking proudly, "If you can trust me without signin' articles, I can trust you for my pay till I've earned it."

Our bargain being concluded and sealed in this high-toned way, I told him to go to a certain well-known nautical outfitting establishment and fit himself out with a complete man-of-war or yacht uniform, whichever suited him best, and have it charged to my account, giving him an order to that effect, and then to get back to the office at 5 o'clock.

At the appointed time, Jack appeared. He had obeyed my instructions to the letter and stood before me, a typical man-of-war's man, as he saluted with his old time grace and informed me that he reported for duty. I took him home with me that afternoon and introduced him to my family. When I explained to them that he was the Jack whose relations to me thirty years before were well known in the household, he was cordially received by everybody and clamorously welcomed by the youngsters, who were delighted at the prospect of having a grown-up sailor in full nautical attire for a companion and mentor in their aquatic sports.

Chapter Twelve ↝

Jack became at once an object of universal interest, not only in our own family and among our visitors and friends, but throughout the neighborhood. His quaint old-fashioned sailor ways; his odd but apt use of nautical terms applied to the various parts of the establishment and to such of the appurtenances and incidents of shore life as he had occasion to mention; his employment of the naval salute on every occasion which in his estimation demanded a display of deference or courtesy; his bluff manners and his rough voice, the gentlest tones of which suggested a gale of wind, combined with his gentleness of heart and the readiness with which an emotion of pain or pleasure caused his tears to flow under the mellowing influence of a glass or two—all contributed to render him a unique character and to win for him the general attention of all classes among our neighbors, and the enthusiastic admiration and affection of all the boys and girls in the village.

I found that time had wrought its changes in Jack, not altogether for the better or the worse, but mainly for the better, so far as morals and habits were concerned. He was a little past thirty in the prime of a sailor's life when I first knew him. He was now over sixty, and sailors under the influence of hardship, exposure, and careless and improvident habits of living age fast. He swore less and drank less, though far from immaculate in either respect. He was religious and devout in his way, although his habits in respect to those two matters would be generally considered deplorably wicked. Otherwise his outward conduct was blameless. These weaknesses he deplored when reminded of their enormity and was always ready to humbly confess and repent of them. Confession to the priest once or twice a month, and to my wife and daughters several times a day, when his breath betrayed his shortcomings in the matter of beer and whiskey, or when his tongue got the better of him, cleared his conscience and made him at peace with himself.

I used to think that, after all, Jack's sins were not at all of the heart, but only of the tongue and throat. When he swore he did not intend the least disrespect or irreverence toward the deities, heathen or Christian, whom he invoked, or cherish the slightest malice toward the individuals or objects, animate or inanimate, whom his tongue sometimes consigned to unmentionable places and unendurable conditions. It was merely a habit of speech as natural and spontaneous, and, let us hope for the repose of his soul, as innocent of wicked or malicious intent, as the singing of a bird.

As to beer and whiskey, they seemed to him as appropriate provisions of nature for physical sustenance as mother's milk, and he imbibed them as guilelessly as in infancy he had absorbed the latter. Unconscious as he was of sin in these indulgences he was quite ready to recognize the repugnance that others might feel concerning them, and to apologize effusively upon the least mention that they were the occasion of offence or grief to his friends.

A day or two after his adoption into the family, he told me that when he shipped he had forgotten to stipulate for a day's liberty now and then for a visit to Clementina who was established in rooms in the city, "just a bit of a stateroom with a cook's galley off," he explained, and who insisted upon this condition in the articles.

"How often, Jack?" I asked.

"Once in two weeks reg'lar, an' maybe an extra now an' agin if ye don't mind," he replied.

I assured him that this was entirely satisfactory, only that it should be once a week, and that he might tell Clementina that the articles should be amended accordingly.

The morning after his return from his first liberty day, I found him sitting on the end of the pier, apparently in great dejection. I sat down beside him and asked him what had gone wrong.

"Ye see, it's this way," he answered, with a very sad note in his voice, "I told Clementina as how I had shipped aboard a gentlemen's country place—a gent as used to be shipmates with me in the *New World*—moored down the bay, an' how 'twas a queer craft with the cook's galley aft, an' the quarterdeck an' ladies cabin forward an' the fo'c'sle aloft (Jack slept in the attic) an' the scuppers in the hold, an' the pump worked with a sail as was the only canvass she carried 'ceptin' quarterdeck awnin's, an' as how I was cox'n of the gig with a boat's crew o' gal kids, an' red velvet cushions to all the thwarts, an' rowlocks an' knees an' rudder yoke all silver, an' tiller ropes made o' silk. She didn't believe a word of it, an' she asked me how long was it sence I thought Clementina Corbett had gone a fool. She said as how she knew there was a woman in it, wotever she meant by that, an' if I was a-goin' to carry on that-a-way, I needn't to come home any more an' I'd better stay with the other one altogether," and Jack's voice broke in a sob and the tears began to flow.

"Never mind, Jack," I said as soothingly as the effort to suppress a laugh would permit. "We'll fix Clementina all right." "Now I'll tell you what to do. Take another day off tomorrow and go and bring her out here. Tell her she's invited with the best compliments of the captain, mate and all hands."

Jack's face brightened, but a look of perplexity still lingered. "Would ye mind givin' it to me in writin' beggin' y'r pardon for

the trouble? She mightn't believe me by word o' mouth seein'
the way she's took in her mind now."

"With the greatest pleasure, Jack, and on gilt-edged paper
with a monogram if you would like."

The idea of the gilt-edged paper seemed to please him
immensely, but I suspected that the monogram puzzled him. In
the morning I called him into the library and wrote the following note:

Mrs. Clementina Corbett

My Dear Madame:

*You are cordially invited to spend the day at our house where we
hope to have the pleasure of your company at the earliest day that
may suit your pleasure and convenience.*

*Your devoted husband, Mr. John Corbett, whom I am proud to call
my friend and former shipmate, and who now holds an honorable
position in my employment, will be the bearer of this and will escort
you to this place whenever it may please you to come.*

Very truly yours,
Alfrederick Smith Hatch and family.

I read it to Jack who expressed the most enthusiastic approval,
and, as he afterwards expressed it, was "that tickled you could
a-knocked me down with a rope yarn."

Then I folded the letter and enclosed it in a large square envelope of the most approved fashionable proportions, addressed it
and handed it to Jack unsealed. He took it gingerly, holding it
by one of the corners between his thumb and one finger. He lingered and fidgeted a minute, a sign that something was on his
mind, not yet clearly settled.

"What is it Jack?" I asked.

"Have ye maybe forgot about that monnygram?" he suggested.

"It's in there, all right, open the letter and see."

"Maybe ye would open it y'self. I might muss it with my awk'ard fingers." I opened it and showed him the monogram at the head of the sheet.

"Is that it?" he asked, looking at it curiously. "It jes' looks like all the knots an' hitches I ever knowed anything about twisted up together."

I carefully traced for him the lines forming the combined initials of my own and my wife's names. He seemed greatly interested.

"Who'd a thought o' that thing spellin' your name an' the missus," he remarked.

I refolded the letter and replaced it in the envelope and handed it back to him. He asked if he "might be so bold as to beg a bit o' waste paper." I gave it to him, when he carefully wrapped it around the letter and placed it in the top of his cap and went away satisfied.

When I got home that afternoon, I found Clementina sitting on the piazza between my wife and eldest daughter with several of the younger children playing around her and climbing over her, and all making much of her, and she looking as happy and contented as a queen.

Jack was fussing about the boathouse a few rods away, occasionally casting furtive glances at the group on the piazza, and apparently in a very satisfied frame of mind.

After being formally introduced to Clementina and exchanging a few words of welcome with her, I sauntered leisurely down the lawn to where Jack was busying himself. As I approached him, he contrived in the performance of what he was pretending to be occupied about, to turn his back toward the house, and as I came up to him he put the forefinger of his right hand against the side of his nose and turning his face partly up to me, winked.

"Well Jack," I said, "It seems to be all serene on the quarter-deck." (This was his nautical name for the piazza.)

He nodded significantly in the direction of the boathouse, and retiring behind it out of sight of the piazza, he called me to him. He approached, and, when we were both concealed from observation, he leaned forward with his hands on his knees and laughed until he was so red in the face I feared he was going to choke. Finally, raising himself up, he put his hand to the side of his mouth toward the house, as if to shut off the sound of his voice in that direction, and between gasps and sobs of suppressed mirth he said in the peculiar hoarse tone which he intended for a whisper, "The letter done it boy, cap'n, I mean, beggin' pardon, the letter done it. She couldn't stand agin that."

Then he told me how when he went to the door of Clementina's apartment, he found it locked, and she, having probably recognized his step in the stairs, refused to open it. After repeated knocking and calling of her name in the sweetest tone his voice was capable of had failed to gain him admittance, he resorted to a stratagem. First he pushed the letter under the door, but it was pushed back again unopened. Then seeing that the transom over the door was partly open, he tossed the letter through the opening, but it came back again by the same road. Then he sat down on the top stair and scratched his head and tried to think it out. Just then the postman came along the street, blowing his whistle at the doors of the houses for which he had letters. Jack hailed him and asked him to come up. Then he induced him to take the letter and blow the whistle at his wife's door, while he concealed himself behind the open door of an adjoining apartment. This ruse succeeded. She took the letter from the postman, and womanly curiosity overcoming her suspicion that after all this might be only a trick of Jack's, she opened and read it. Then with a flushed face she ran out into the hall and called, "Jack Corbett, you come here." Jack came sheepishly from behind the door and confronted her with a look on his face that was probably something like a cross between a cunning smile of triumph and the whimper of a schoolboy caught in the act.

"Look here, Jack Corbett, are you foolin' me?"

"How could I fool ye that way when ye know well enough as I can't write a word o' any kind o' scrawl, much less a work o' art like that," he answered.

"But you might ha' got some other fool to write it," said Clementina in a tone that was half accusing, half enquiring.

"I hasn't got nobody to write nothing 'cept his honor hi'self, an' he ain't no fool," Jack replied with spirit, feeling that he must stand up for me whatever might come of it. "It's genooine, Clementina, it's genooine, sure's my name's John Corbett."

After some more parleying, Clementina surrendered, and the scene on the piazza was the result. Clementina stayed to dinner and, with great difficulty, after much scrubbing of his hands, oiling and combing of his hair and whiskers, polishing of his shoes and dusting of his uniform, my oldest daughter on one side and I on the other, succeeded in half coaxing, half dragging him into the dining room to sit at the table with her and the family. We made him sit down between one of the older girls and Clementina, where his attitude and expression of mingled pride, mischief, shamefacedness, and awkwardness were funny to see. His response reminded me of numerous occasions when, as a boy in the district school, I had been compelled as a punishment to go and sit among the girls for flirting with them on the opposite side of the school room. Under Clementina's watchful eye, and with occasional admonitory nudges from her elbows, Jack succeeded in handling his knife and fork in a fairly correct manner and in carrying himself generally through the unaccustomed ordeal with credit to himself and without greatly shocking Clementina's sense of propriety.

Jack escorted her home later in the evening and returned next morning in his most placid and contented humor. He performed his duties throughout the day with a cheerful alacrity that spoke volumes for the condition in which he had left things at headquarters. When he thought himself alone and unobserved, he would wag his head and chuckle to himself in great apparent glee. He took occasion to say to me, "When she see as 'twas all true just as I tol' her an' no foolin', she did the 'ansome thing an' axed my pardon fair an' square like a lady, an' Clementina is a lady if she do git high strung and skittish now an' agin. "

We never heard that there was thereafter any interruption to the smooth flow of the current of Jack's domestic bliss.

When Jack's first month of service was up, I handed him thirty dollars for his month's pay, which was what had been agreed upon. He gave back five dollars.

"What is this for, Jack?" I asked.

"To pay for the sov'r'n I got away with in Liverpool, yer honor," he answered, in as matter of fact a tone as if the voyage had been six months instead of thirty years before.

"How about the interest," I said, to have a little fun with him.

"Wot's that, yer honor?"

"Why, Jack, don't you know that when a man borrows money he expects to pay interest on it? The rate of interest in New York State is seven percent, and as our ship hailed from New York the laws of that state would govern in a financial transaction on her deck. You see that don't you, Jack?"

He nodded his head and looked wise, as if the problem was as clear to him as the North Star in a cloudless night.

"Well," I went on, "money at seven percent simple interest doubles itself once in a little over fourteen years and, at compound interest, once in about 10 years. It is thirty years since you borrowed that sovereign. Now if you will take your log book and pencil and figure it out you will find that it has grown to about twenty-one dollars at simple interest, and to about forty dollars at compound interest."

Again he looked wise, with his head on one side, as if following me with a deep mental calculation, like a lightning calculator, but with a puzzled expression rather having the mastery. "Wal'," he said at last, "I guess yer honor's right 'ithout me figgerin' it out," and he handed me back the remaining twenty-five dollars. "An' I'll pay ye the rest out o' next month's wages."

"You won't do any such thing," I said, thrusting the whole back into his hand to his astonishment. "Don't think I am going to take almost a month and a half's pay out of an old shipmate who did so much for me. I was only fooling with you a bit, Jack." But having thus thoughtlessly put it into his head that he owed me a sovereign and thirty years' compound interest, it was not so easy to get it out of his head again; and, for several months after that, I had to have it out with him every time I offered him his wages.

The girls had a one-horse phaeton with a rumble behind in which they used to drive about the village and surrounding country. One day it pleased their fancy to ask Jack to go in the rumble in his uniform. As they drove off Jack leaned forward in the rumble with his arms and hands in position as if holding a pair of tiller ropes. His body swayed this side and that as if to get a clear lookout ahead, and accommodating itself to the motion of the vehicle, it rose and fell and swayed with the inequalities of the road, like a boat in a seaway. He seemed to be under the impression that he was steering the craft and that it was his duty to keep it clear of rocks and shoals and to avoid collision with the numerous other craft that thronged the roadstead. His unusual attitude and strange livery attracted general attention along the road, which Jack felt it incumbent on him to acknowledge with the usual salutes to right and left. This, with proper attention to the tiller ropes and to the course, kept him very busy. It was some time before the young ladies discovered the cause of the unusual attention and suppressed merriment of which their turnout seemed to be the object.

"Is anything the matter with the harness?" suggested one.

"Or with my hat?" queried the other.

"Is my dress all right behind?" asked the first, observing that the looks and smiles of the passersby seemed to be directed to the rear of their establishment.

Finally, looking back, they discovered Jack in his attitude of a coxswain steering a boat in a treacherous or crowded channel, with his right hand rapidly alternating between the starboard tiller rope and his cap in the combined duties of steering and saluting.

"Sit up straight, Jack," said the elder.

"Fold your arms, Jack," commanded the other.

"Yes, miss," he answered to each, as he obeyed these orders with something of an injured air, as if submitting to the demands of discipline against his own judgment.

When they reached a retired part of the road, the girls got out of the phaeton and put Jack through a drill in the proper attitude for duty in the rumble. An hour later they drove into the yard with Jack sitting up as straight as is possible for an old sailor, his arms folded across his breast, with a dejected and humiliated air, as if he felt himself a prisoner in manacles. His cap had got tipped on one side of his head in a jaunty and dissipated looking way by the jolting of the carriage. He had evidently been afraid to disobey orders by unfolding his arms long enough to set it straight.

"Wot's the good of a cox'n settin' in the starn sheets straight

on end like a blarsted marine as has swallered a bundle o' ram-
rods, with his arms folded an' his flippers no more use'n a dead
whale's an' them gals a drivin' her like mad in a narrer channel
an' like to be run down any minit by one o' them lubberly mud
scows or clam diggers?" was his comment when telling me
about it afterwards.

I had earnestly charged Jack to keep a close watch over the
younger children when they were bathing or playing about the
water, and on no account to let one of them get drowned. I
assured him, numerous as they were, there were none to spare,
and warned him in the most impressive manner that I held him
responsible for their safety.

He had pledged himself with equal impressiveness that he
himself would perish before one of them should come to harm
while under his eye. No anxious hen ever watched with greater
solicitude the brood of young ducklings she had been beguiled
into hatching, as she saw them take to the water, than was
bestowed by Jack upon the young water sprites committed to
his charge. He spliced the handle of a boat hook to twice its
original length and kept it handy as a means of promptly fishing them out when they accidentally fell overboard or insisted
on wading beyond their depth. One day after the frail belt of
ribbon around the waist of one of them had given way as she was
suspended in the air at the end of the boat hook, leaving her to
fall back sprawling into the water, he set to work and made for
each of them a strong canvas belt to buckle round the waist,
with a loop made of rope at the back—a "becket" he called it,
the sailor name for such an attachment. He insisted they should
wear the belt whenever they were going near the water.

This contrivance, he assured me with much satisfaction, was
strong enough to "h'ist a young whale aboard." Jack was so
proud of his life-saving device, and so fond of bringing it into
use, that he would upon the slightest pretext of danger reach

out with the boat hook, dexterously insert the prong into the becket, and deposit a sprawling youngster on the float. After that it was no uncommon thing, upon hearing a splash followed by a childish yell, to look up from one's newspaper or book and see a dripping object, like a large frog in child's clothing, suspended by the middle at the end of the boat hook, with arms and legs hanging down and feet and hands beating the air. The children themselves considered it great sport, and would often, when wading or bathing, suddenly, with a great splash, cry out. "Oh! Jack, I'm drowning; fish me out quick."

They took particular delight in watching their opportunity to catch Jack off his guard. When his back was turned for a minute, they would make an unusually vigorous splash and splutter, just to see him rush to the rescue, and, when landed on the float, they would feign insensibility at first, and then come to with a few gasps, and solemnly reproach him with, "Oh! Jack, I came awfully near drowning that time." When his face would grow long or the tears start, they would jump up with a laugh and say,

"Oh! I'm all right now. Thank you, dear Jack, for saving my life."

Once there was real danger. One of them who had just learned to swim a little was eager to show off before the others and struck out beyond her depth. When, after a few convulsive strokes, she felt with her feet for the bottom and did not find it, she lost her head, swallowed a few mouthfuls of salt water in attempting to cry out, and sank until only her hair floated on the surface. Jack ran to the outer end of the float and reached for her with the boat hook, but she had got beyond its length. The tide was going out, and every second took her a little farther away.

Jack could not swim, but he did not hesitate. With a look on his face that suggested both the sublime purpose of self-sacrifice and a silent appeal for help that glorified its rugged lineaments as with the reflection of an invisible halo, he plunged in. To his surprise and relief he brought up with his feet on bottom in water a little over breast high. He had retained the boat hook which he now thrust forward to its full length, but it fell short. Then he waded toward the mass of floating hair which showed where the child was still supported near the surface by her garments, the water deepening at every step. Now it covered his shoulders; in a moment more, it was closing around his throat; in another it was up to his chin. Just as the wavelets began to lap about his mouth, held high with his head back, the boat hook caught. Stepping quickly back to where the water receded to his shoulders again, he drew her to him, and, raising her head above the water, towed her to the float and laid her now limp and inanimate form gently on it and climbed out after her.

The unconsciousness was not feigned this time; and there was no mock fright and sham weeping among the scared group of youthful spectators. It was the real thing now. Jack took her up in his arms and started toward the house. By this time the screams of the younger ones had brought their mother to the door, and as she came flying in terror down the lawn, Jack met her and laid the child in her outstretched arms and said in his simple way, the tears running down his cheeks and his voice broken with sobs, "I 'ope she ain't drownded, Mar'm, I done my best so 'elp me God."

Then he followed the mother with her dripping burden to the house and sitting down on the piazza steps, buried his face in his hands and continued to cry piteously. He resisted all efforts to induce him to change his wet clothing, and could not be persuaded to leave his post until word was brought to him that the young lady had revived and was all right. Then he rose to his feet, drew the back of his hand across his eyes, and, in a half-dazed way, went slowly to his forecastle at the top of the house.

He appeared half an hour later in dry clothing, but with a very solemn expression on his face. He was evidently not thinking of his successful rescue of the child so much as he was reproaching himself for the peril she had incurred while under his care; and he seemed bowed down with an impression that he was going to be court-martialed and dismissed from the service in disgrace, or hanged at the yardarm, and that he deserved his fate.

When the children caught sight of him, they flocked around him, climbed up on him behind, before, and on both sides, put their arms around his neck, patted his cheeks, stroked his whiskers, kissed him and lavished all manner of endearments on him, much to his surprise and embarrassment.

They called him "dear Jack," "brave Jack," and all the sweet names they could think of. One little creature, seeing the tears this unexpected demonstration had set flowing again, rolling down his cheeks, dabbed them with her chubby hands and pleaded, "Poor Jack, don't cry any more. Sister wasn't drowned a bit, and she has waked up all right." As this precious little comforter had been engaged in making mud pies on the shore when the excitement occurred, and everybody had been too much preoccupied since to think of washing her hands, her kind offices in wiping away Jack's tears left on his cheeks the appearance of an Indian in his war paint.

While this was still going on, a message came that Jack was wanted in the house. He went timidly into the hall and followed with a hesitating step the beckoning servant to the sitting room where the resuscitated miss was lying on a lounge with the air of a person who had suddenly emerged from the dead level usually pertaining to a family of eleven, to the distinction of being the principal object of interest. She bade Jack approach with something of the manner of a queen about to confer the honors of knighthood on a subject who had acquitted himself well in some conspicuous affair.

She had a very distinct notion, this romantic young miss, as to what was the correct thing in deportment for a self-respecting young woman toward a male person of inferior station who might have the good fortune to be instrumental in saving her life. As this was her first opportunity, and might be her last, for reducing it to practice, she had evidently determined to make the most of it. As he shyly drew near, she held out a hand to him. He took it in his rough paw and began to shake it gently and then to pat it with his other hand. "You may kiss it, Jack," she said; and he kissed it reverently. Then, suddenly as a summer squall bursts from a quiet sky, her air of queenly dignity and her prearranged plan went all to pieces, and springing half up from her reclining posture with a great sob, she caught him around the neck with both arms and drew his face down to hers and kissed him, first on one rugged cheek and then on the other. At this the fountains of the great deep of Jack's tender emotions were broken up afresh, and their tears mingled together on her dainty wrapper and his rough shirt.

When the older boys came home from school and the city, and heard the story, they slapped Jack on the back one after the other and told him he was a "trump" and a "brick" and a "bully boy" and a "brave old son-of-a-gun," and various other things to which they gave characteristic boyish appellations of distinction.

When I stepped off the train from the city later in the afternoon, I found myself surrounded by nearly the whole brood of clamorous youngsters, who, circling me in my walk toward the house with dancing feet and noisy tongues, attempted to give me all at once their separate versions of what had happened. If I had not had, all around me, such palpable evidence that they were all very much alive, I might have thought at first that the whole family had been drowned in ten fathoms of water, that Jack had fished them all up with boat hooks, and that they were all at that moment lying on lounges with pallid cheeks and dripping garments, waiting to come to and tell me how it felt. Before we reached the house, however, I had gathered out of the confused babble a fairly coherent idea of what had really taken place.

After kissing and congratulating the rescued young lady, I sought Jack and expressed to him my gratitude and appreciation, and assured him that if I were only Emperor of France he should be decorated with the medal of the Legion of Honor. Jack's emotions on finding himself suddenly transformed from a self-convicted criminal into a hero, and the odd mixture of humility and pride with which they were manifested, cannot be described.

Chapter Thirteen ✍

The older girls had taken upon themselves the task of reforming Jack in respect to his two besetting sins. They gave him long and earnest lectures on the wickedness of profanity, and quoted to him all the scripture on the subject that a diligent study of Crudens Concordance revealed, dwelling particularly on the third commandment. They also warned him against the evils of drink and the dreadful consequences that lurked in the intoxicating cup. They plied him with scripture quotations on this point also, and the most solemn assurances, on the authority of inspiration, that no drunkard could possibly go to Heaven, and that the seductive liquids he imbibed were cunningly contrived devices of the Evil One to drag him down to hell.

Sundays afforded great opportunity for their pious labors on Jack's behalf and for wrestling with the twin spirits of evil they sought to cast out of him. On this day, boating, fishing, swimming, and other secular pursuits that kept them and Jack very busy on weekdays, were suspended. When time hung heavy on their hands between church and Sunday school and meals, and their restless vitality thirsted for something to do, they would swoop down on Jack as he peacefully smoked his pipe at the end of the pier or in some secluded corner of the grounds, and vigorously attack these enemies of his soul. On these occasions the usual makeup of a Sunday school class, with one teacher and several scholars, was reversed, and one very meek scholar submitted to three or half a dozen lively and voluble teachers sitting around him in a semicircle on the grass or on boat cushions spread on the pier or float.

They would exhort him with great zeal and earnestness, and when quoting to him some particularly blood-curdling extract from temperance lecture or sermon concerning the fate of the drunkard or profane swearer, they would sink their voices to a sepulchral tone intended to strike him with terror. They would emphasize it all with ominous pointing of their fingers at him, which Jack would contemplate with something of the air with which he might be expected to view a cordon of bayonets fixed for his execution.

To all this Jack gave the most humble and respected attention, nodding his head in solemn approval of the sentiments expressed or wagging it seriously in recognition of the unanswerable force of their arguments and admonitions. These silent responses would be interspersed with an occasional "Yes, Miss" or "Sartin, Miss."

Frequently, and with appalling emphasis, they would put the question, "Where do you think you will go to when you die if you keep on swearing and drinking?" He would answer with meek resignation, "I dun'no, Miss, 'cept maybe 'twere that hell-fire place an' that there lake o' brimstone the priest tells about, or maybe they'll let me off with a good long spell o' purgatory, seein' as I hain't never killed a body, only p'r'aps 'twere accidental-like in battle, an' never shirked my duty aboard ship, nor deserted in the face o' the enemy. Don't you think maybe they'll count them things in a bit agin' the drinkin' an' the swearin' considerin' it's only an old sailor as hain't had no sort o' pious trainin'?"

Once, in a grave tone, as if considering a very serious and perplexing problem, but with a cunning sideways glance out of the corner of his eye, he asked one of them, "I say, miss, if ye don't mind answerin' an ignorant old feller's questions as may be only jes' foolishness, where do ye s'pose they'll git all the brimstone from to keep that there lake a-goin to all etarnity? I've sometimes kind o' hoped as may be if the devil did git old Jack after all, spite o' the priest an' Clementina an' you, the stuff would a-gin out afore I got thar."

Five pairs of hands were raised in horror and five awe-stricken voices exclaimed in chorus, "Oh, Jack." But Jack looked as innocent as if he had only asked how it was "them alligators didn't eat Moses when he was a-sleepin' in the bulrushes."

Another time, apparently a little wearied with the monotony of the exclusive application of scripture to his own case, he sought to create a diversion by a sudden allusion to Jonah and the whale. "Do ye mind tellin' me that story about a chap—I don't jes' remember his name, as was swallered by a whale?"

He listened attentively to the story and when it was finished he meditated a while, and then asked, "It's in the Bible, ain't it?"

"Yes, Jack, it's in the Bible."

"An' the Bible's all true I suppose?"

"Yes, Jack."

"Well then, I s'pose I've got ter b'lieve that story along o' the rest, but it's a tough un—aye it's a tough un." And then, after a moment's reflection, "S'pose if 'twere in the Bible as that Jonah chap swallered the whale I'd have ter b'lieve it all the same."

"What makes it so hard to believe that the whale swallowed Jonah, Jack?" asked one.

"Well you see, Miss, it's this way. Sailors likes to know as everything's all fair an' square as laid down on the charts. So we takes soundin's, an' if the soundin's agrees with the chart, well an' good. If not, we has ter go by the soundin's, 'cause, ye see, Miss, we couldn't afford ter run the ship aground in three fathom o' water when she was drawin' three an' a half, jes' because the chart said as there was four fathom, an' the soundin's only showed three where we was, an' a-shoalin' all the time. So we downs helm an' goes about for deep water, spite o' the chart."

"What has that got to do with the whale swallowing Jonah?" she asked.

"Well, I'll tell you, Miss. One time when I was aboard a whaler in the Ar'tic seas, we had a chap in the fo'c'sle as had been a parson afore he was broke for preachin' of a Sunday when he was drunk. He used to say as how they didn't mind him a snap o' their fingers gittin' drunk 'cause all the parsons 'round them parts where he come from, he said, used to be as jolly as a man-o'-war's crew on liberty most o' the time o' weekdays, only they had to sober up for funerals and for preachin' of a Sunday. An' when one time he had such a lovely drunk onto him as he couldn't bear to let go on it an' start in all over agin a Monday mornin' an' tried to carry it over Sunday, they got mad an' give him his discharge without papers. When he couldn't git another job o' preachin', he shipped afore the mast in a whaler, as was the next best thing he could do.

"He had been preachin' so long, an' the habit of it was so set in him, he couldn't keep his jaw off it, an' so he kept it a goin' in the foc's'le an' what with preachin' an' cussin' an' drinkin' an' fightin', he was the curiousest critter as I was ever shipmates with. Well, he had the Bible at his tongue's end as handy as any old sailor boxin' the compass, an' he used to tell all them queer stories about the donkey as talked back, an' the chap as slewed a whole regiment wi' the jawbone o' one o' 'em—don't rightly remember if that there jawbone belonged to the same donkey as did the talking—an' about the little feller as knocked over a giant four times bigger'n him with just a bit of a stone an' a sling, an' a lot more o' the same sort. But when he come to that there whale story there was them as had been handling whales all their lives an' thought as that was something they ort ter know a bit about, leastways as much as any parson or any land-lubber writin' a book ashore as had never seed a whale; an' they stuck to it as no whale was ever harpooned as could swaller a man whole. The parson he stuck to it as 'twere in the Bible, an' the Bible were true, every word. An' so, after a lot o' jawin' about it, they made it up atween 'em as the next time we had a big whale alongside, they'd prove wot was the right of it.

"Next day after this 'greement was come to, we struck a two hund'd bar'l whale, an' afore night we had him alongside. As the weather was fine an' no change threat'nin', the cap'n he give out as we wouldn't begin cuttin' in till next mornin', so we had a good chance o' findin' out' bout that swallerin' bus'nis. Now you see, Miss, a whale hain't got no hinges to his upper jaw, an' the only way to git at his mouth was to lift his head clean out o' the water an' let his under jaw drop down. So we rigged a tops'l hal-yards 'round him just abaft his lower jaw an' rove it through a block on the fore yardarm, an' then takin' it to the main deck caps'n we hove on it 'till we had his nose a p'intin' 'bout the same way as the flyin' jib boom, an' his mouth wide open.

"It'd been made up as a sailor named Bill Thom'son was to have a line made fast to him an' be let down into the whale's mouth an' see how fur he could git. It was agreed as how when he fetched up agin' anything, an' couldn't git no further, or if he found hi'self a slippin' down too fur an' got afeared he was a goin' plum inter the critter's belly sure enough, he was to give a jark on the line an' then we was to haul him out. He'd been the biggest talker agin a whale havin' a hole in his for'ard port big enough to let a man in, but he was nigh weak'nin' when it come to the scratch, an' he wanted us all to sw'ar as we'd pull like hell."

"Hush, Jack," admonished one of the girls.

"Beggin' your pardon, Miss, them's 'is words, not mine—pull like hell, quick as ever he jarked on the line. He warn't satisfied 'till the parson stood us all up in a row an' sw'ared us, an' made us kiss the book all 'round. Ther' warn't no Bible in the fo'c'sle, but Bill he pulled out a book about a feller named Gulliver, or something like that, as had traveled all 'round, which he said was the truest book next to the Bible as he knowed about, an' we all kissed that.

"Then we made the line fast 'round Bill under his arms, an lowered away han'somely. When he got so fur we could only jest see the top o' his head an' we thought as he was a goin' clean out o' sight, he jarked the line an' we hauled him up. Bill he swore, an' kissed the book on it, as he couldn't only git one leg down that thar whale's throat, an' 'twas that tight it pulled his boot off when we hauled him out; an' sure's we be settin' here, miss, when we come to look one o' his boots was gone.

"Now ye see, Miss, how an old sailor as has been a whalin' an' knows a bit about th' critters, couldn't b'lieve that thar Jonah yarn if it warn't in th' Bible, 'cause it don't agree with th' soundin's." And Jack shook his head with an air of pious resignation to the duty of believing whatever was in the Bible whether it agreed with the soundings or not.

Having been an interested listener to this part of the talk, I asked Jack how the parson explained the discrepancy between the Bible story and the soundings.

"Ye see, cap,'n, we was a talkin' it over in the fo'c's'le, an' the parson he goes on to tell us as how ther' was a law o' nature that when a thing warn't no kind o' use no more, it kind o' dried up. He said as how we was all monkeys or rangotangs once an' had tails a fathom long as was handy in hanging' on to limbs o' trees an' such like, but when the woods was cleared away, an' we came to live on th' ground an' in houses, an' set down on chairs, an' wear clothes, th' tails warn't no use after that but th'd only be in th' way, an' so they kind o' shrunked up bit by bit 'till thar warn't nothing left of 'em.

"One o' the men said he thought they might a left 'em on them as was goin' to be sailors, 'cause they'd come handy goin' aloft an' holdin' on an' warkin' with both hands in a gale o' wind. But the parson he said that wouldn't do, 'cause some o' them as had tails left onto 'em mightn't conclude to go to sea after all, an' they'd only be in the way an' git trod on, an' then ag'in, some o' them others might want to take to a seafarin' life, an' they wouldn't have a fair show."

"But what did that have to do with Jonah and the whale?"

"Well, the parson said as how whales when they was fust made had to have big throats 'cause they lived mostly on men an' other big fish, an' everything was bigger in them days, an' when that thar whale swallered Jonah 'twas a long time ago afore the'r throats had had time to shrink much of any to speak of. But after a while they couldn't git anything to eat but little fish an' crabs an' somethin' he called crustashuns 'cause the sharks had got made then an' they was livelier, 'n the whales hadn't no more use for th'er big throats, but they was ruther a' onconvenience to 'em 'cause they couldn't feel the little critters they lived on goin' down, an' couldn't git no sort o' enjoyment out o' tastin' of 'em; an so th'r throats had been shrinkin' ever sence. He said 'twas a wonder to him, now as he'd come to think it over, how Bill's big foot could a got down that thar whale's throat alongside, consid'rin' all the time it'd had ter shrink sence Jonah were swallered."

When I suggested that sperm whales had teeth and ample throats, and were said to make away with the biggest kind of sea squids in two or three bites, and that it might have been a sperm whale that swallowed Jonah, he replied, "Well, yer honor, a whale's a whale, an' a sparm whale's a sparm whale—nother kind o' critter entirely. I'm thinkin' as how if th' Bible had

meant 'twas a sparm whale as swallowed that Jonah feller it'd a
said so, beggin' yer honor's pardon. That ship as I was tellin' of
was in the Ar'tic Seas huntin' right whales, an' 'twere that kind
as th' parson an' the crew knowed about, an' they hain't got no
kind o' throats with openin's as th' soundin's shewed."

Jack related all this with the utmost gravity and apparent sin-
cerity, but whether there was a grain of truth in the story, or
whether it was only a cunningly devised fable to divert attention from the application of scripture to his own shortcomings,
and to use up the time until the dinner bell should call off his
teachers, it was impossible to say.

The children were greatly disturbed by the idea that a whale's
throat was not large enough to swallow a man, as it seemed to
strike at the foundations of their hitherto implicit belief in the
literal truth of all the Bible stories. At the dinner table they
demanded to know what I thought about it. I was obliged to
confess that I hadn't the least idea that an ordinary whale such
as Jack referred to ever could have swallowed Jonah, and that I
considered the explanation of Jack's parson shipmate utterly
absurd. This made them still more downcast, until I relieved
their minds by assuring them that the word translated "whale"
in the story of Jonah, did not necessarily mean Jack's kind of a
whale at all, but only a big fish of some kind. They were much
relieved.

When, however, they tried this solution of the problem on
Jack, he gravely shook his head, and when they backed it up
with what was to them the conclusive statement, "Papa said so,"
he remarked, "Maybe the cap'n's right. He's mostly th' rightest
man I ever knowed, but to my way o' thinkin' a whale's a whale,
an' when the Bible says a whale it means a whale an' nothin'
else. I reckon the parson was right about the shrinkin'.
Howsomever that may be though, all you an' old Jack's got to
do's jes' to b'lieve as somehow th' Bible's true."

After each of these determined efforts on the part of the girls for Jack's reformation, ending as they invariably did with the most solemn promises on his part that he would never drink nor swear any more, qualified by the saving clause, which he never forgot to insert, "not if I can 'elp it, Miss," they would feel much elated in the belief that their labors had been crowned with success at last. This cheerful conviction would last until the escape of a refractory fish of unusual promise as to size from Jack's hook, or the perplexing and inextricable entanglement of a crab in the meshes of the crabbing net, or some other untoward event, would send his good resolutions flying down the wind and let loose the brood of imprecations that seemed to be always lurking under his tongue to take him unawares. Or until, returning from his visit to the city on his next liberty day, a powerful odor of beer and whiskey pervading the atmosphere wherever he appeared, would proclaim a relapse and dash their hopes.

Despairing finally of the lasting efficacy of verbal promises they determined to get him down in black and white.

"Can you write your name, Jack?" they asked one day.

"No, Miss, but I can make my mark as tidy as th' next one, an' that has sarved my turn for writin' ever sence I signed articles for my first voyage, which was out o' Cork nigh on fifty year ago."

That night, I found the four oldest girls in the library, one of them at the desk pen in hand and fingers very much inked, and the others sitting around, all apparently in very solemn conclave. They ordered me out of the room peremptorily with the information that they were engaged in important business and must not be disturbed on any pretext.

The following evening, they triumphantly submitted for my inspection a document of which the following is a copy:

I, John Corbett, mariner, hereby solemnly promise and agree that I will not hereafter drink any more beer, ale, wine, whiskey or any other intoxicating beverages of any kind whatsoever; and that I will not swear any more.

His

John　　　***X***　　　***Corbett***

Mark

P.S. Except that I may have a pint of beer with Clementina on liberty days, and no more.

The original draft had contained only the first clause; but Jack had pleaded hard for a concession in favor of two pints of beer on liberty days. After a long and animated discussion, a compromise on one pint was effected and embodied in the postscript.

The effect of this written pledge seemed to be more enduring than any previous measures for Jack's reformation, and the girls were happy accordingly. It was several weeks before he was heard by any of them to swear. It was noticed that frequently, when anything occurred calculated to irritate him, he would suddenly drop whatever he was occupied about, and, with set teeth and a very red face, hastily retire inside the boathouse or barn, or behind a convenient clump of shrubbery, and remain in seclusion for several minutes.

It was taken for granted that at these times Jack was wrestling in secret with the temptation to swear, and that the placid temper in which he reappeared gave evidence that he had come off victorious. These moments of retirement were, therefore, respected accordingly, and were looked upon by the girls with something like awe.

Once, however, one of the boys—an irreverent young imp—whose curiosity got the better of his respect for Jack's desire to be alone, succeeded in getting, by a circuitous route among the bushes, in close proximity to the clump behind which Jack had concealed himself. According to his account afterwards, he heard what made his hair stand on end. It thus became known that Jack's wrestlings were of quite another sort than had been supposed, and that he was evidently acting on the principle that the tendency to swear, like poison in the blood, had better come out on the surface than be bottled up or driven in. When this was reported to Jack's horrified mentors, and he was called to account by them for having violated his pledge, he seemed greatly surprised and hurt. The sin had, according to his perceptions, consisted so entirely in the offence that strong language gave to others, that he felt he was living up to his promise like a man when he did all his swearing by himself and denied himself the luxury of giving vent to his feelings in public.

For some time, also, there seemed to be a marked improvement in the matter of drink. The sharpest little nose failed to detect any objectionable odor in the atmosphere about Jack, except on his return from the city after a day's liberty; and then no one could say that it was more than was reasonably due to his privileged pint of beer. On these occasions, after giving account of himself in his usual guileless way, he was subjected to a sharp cross examination accompanied with frequent and vigorous sniffings and keen investigations as to the condition of his breath that might indicate anything stronger than beer.

The time came, alas, when there was no mistaking the evidence that Jack had fallen from grace. The odor of whiskey, mingling with that of beer, gave him hopelessly away to the sensitive nostrils of his youthful guardians.

"Jack, you have been drinking," said one of them as soon as he came within smelling distance on his return from the city one afternoon.

"Only the pint of beer, Miss," he asserted stoutly.

"Whiskey, Jack, don't pretend to deny it. Your breath tells the story," she insisted, turning her face away with a grimace.

"'Twas only a nip, Miss, only a nip," he pleaded.

"More than that, Jack, four nips at least; you may as well own up to it," she insisted again, stamping her foot.

Jack could never stand long against this sort of demonstration on her part; and his courage and effrontery oozed away all at once, and left him a crestfallen culprit.

"Well, Miss, I'll tell ye the truth, 'twere two."

"Stop, Jack, don't tell any more lies. It's bad enough as it is to keep you awake nights for a fortnight. And what will Papa say?"

Jack shook in his shoes at the implied threat. The perspiration came out in big drops on his forehead and neck.

"Now see here, Missy, don't ye go to tellin' 'im, an' I'll tell ye all about it. 'Twere jest three nips, an' not another one, so 'elp me God, an' 'twas this way. When I'd had my reg'lar pint with Clementina after supper 'cordin' to law, I up anchor an' laid my course for th' ferry. When I was crossin' West Street, an' luffin' an' yawin' to part an' starb'd to steer clear o' them lubberly hoss cars an' other land craft, first I knowed I was hit in the I 'ead an' didn't see nothin' but about a million stars all blue, an' red, an' yeller, a dancin' 'round me like a dozen o' them corposants that comes an' sits on the spars sometimes at sea, all flyin' in pieces. When I come to, I was a layin' on th' floor in th' saloon on th' corner an some chaps was a leanin' over me an' one was a tin-kerin' my head which felt like a shell had busted inside of it. I felt something a running down my throat, an' when I got my taste, I knowed 'twere whiskey. Now ye see, Miss, 'twere agin' nature for an old sailor as loves whiskey to interfere when 'twere a running right inter him nat'ral like 'ithout any doing o' his, 'specially when his head was a humming like a log reel running off ten knots, an' no more sense into it than a biled lobster's. Well when I comed to an' opened my eyes, they kind o' stopped pouring, an' I kind o' missed it o' course. Then I shet my eyes an' made b'live to go off agin. Yer see, Miss, I warn't rightly m'self, an' wot with th' buzzing in my head an' th' feeling o' th' whiskey, I disremembered all about that thar pledge, an' when th' doctor he said to give me some more, I didn't resist—I confess to it, Miss—I didn't resist, but jes' took in all they had a mind to gi' me. I thought as how the doctor knowed best wot were good for me, an' 'twould be onbeocomin' in me to interfere.

"After a while, they got me onto my feet, an' then I was that dazed an' upset. I didn't know th' bar from th' sidewalk, an' when an old sailor as had been lookin' said, 'Look a-here, mate 'ave another to kind o' stiddy ye'self.' An' the bartender he set down a big tumbler full o' something an' I jes' swallered it as a matter o' course 'ithout considering. Them were th' three nips, Miss, the' were big ones, I don't pretend to deny, but the' were only three. Then the policeman he put me aboard the boat, an' that's all I knows about it."

In confirmation of this remarkable story, Jack pulled off his cap and showed a cut about an inch and a half long across one side of his head a little above the ear, drawn together by three or four narrow strips of fresh sticking plaster. The cut was an indisputable fact. But how much of the rest of the story was true, or which had been the cause and which the effect, the cut or the whiskey, we never discovered. Jack stuck, with a constancy that could not be shaken, to his original story, but there was, at times, a suspicion in the family that he had somehow got the cart before the horse, and that the whiskey came first and the cut afterwards.

The demoralizing effect of a broken pledge was exemplified in Jack's case. It has been generally observed that when a man takes a pledge, or publicly announces a good resolution, and breaks it, a collapse of his moral backbone for the time being is almost certain to follow. The consciousness of weakness and the shame of it, take the nerve out of him. And the loss of confidence in the strength of his purpose and will induces the recklessness of discouragement which finds expression in the oft repeated, "It's no use to try." This moral degradation is usually in proportion to the formality with which the pledge has been taken and the publicity given to its existence and its breach. And thus the very conditions which are designed to add to its value as a restraining force, render the consequences of breaking it more fatal, just as the explosion of a shell is more destructive the greater the strength and resistance of the material of which it is composed. The operation of this principle in Jack's case seemed to cast serious doubt on his account of the accidental and involuntary character of his indulgence in the "three nips." If there was no sense of moral responsibility for it, or of voluntary violation of his pledge, it was hard to understand its demoralizing effect. With the parting of the line that held him to the written instrument to which he had affixed his mark—that sign which to illiterate people often seems to have a mysterious significance and a sacredness greater even than that of a written signature to some better educated persons—all his moorings seemed to be cast loose, and the girls sorrowfully beheld, as they thought, the results of their painstaking labor for his moral reconstruction going to hopeless wreck. For some time after this, the "nips" were frequent, with hardly an attempt at disguise, and he no longer took the trouble to seek the seclusion of the boathouse or the bushes, when he felt his tongue breaking loose.

After a few days of despairing inaction, during which they felt like exclaiming with the prophet, "Ephraim is joined to his idols; let him alone," they braced up, and, with characteristic persistence, returned to the attack. As the result of frequent mysterious and solemn councils of war, which, when held at the end of the pier or out on their boat or elsewhere, in Jack's sight but out of his hearing, he eyed suspiciously, they decided on an entirely new system of tactics. Tongue and pen and serious measures having failed, they determined to try pantomime and ridicule.

The day after this conclusion was reached was liberty day for Jack, and they perfected their plans for putting their new system into effect on his return from the city. They added to their forces by enlisting the two youngest boys. The boys had affected to make light of the girls' moral efforts with Jack. They even goaded Jack to profanity. Sometimes they purposely tangled their fishing lines or hid the oars of the girls' boat when they were about to order it put in readiness for a row. They did this just for the amusement of hearing him swear and to witness the girls' chagrin; therefore, they entered with alacrity into the girls' scheme because they scented fun in it.

When Jack appeared toward night, he was met near the gate and surrounded by eight speechless pantomimists sniffing at him with upturned noses and significantly gesticulating with their arms. When he had come near enough for the telltale odors to become apparent, eight indignant noses were seized between the thumbs and forefingers of eight right hands, while the palms of eight left hands were pressed against a like number of seemingly rebellious stomachs, and eight usually jolly faces were distorted with a variety of grimaces intended to express disgust and approaching nausea.

Jack had braced himself, as usual, for a verbal onslaught and for stoutly insisting that he had done nothing amiss, or that it was "only a nip," and had fortified himself with a plausible yarn to account for whatever delinquencies he might be forced to confess. But he was wholly unprepared for this novel method of moral reform. It took him aback and, as he expressed it afterwards, "knocked me clean out o' my reck'nin'."

Jack, as we have seen, was glib enough with his tongue when occasion required, and generally had a ready answer to anything expressed in words, but in the presence of this dumb show he was dumb. He looked on in amazement, while successive expressions of perplexity and pain chased each other across his troubled face, as he sidled off the boardwalk to the middle of the carriage drive. Here he stood irresolute for a minute, fumbling his cap between his hands and shuffling his feet uneasily, and then suddenly he made a bolt in the direction of the boathouse with the whole pack at his heels, never slacking his pace nor looking back until he reached it and shut and bolted himself in.

All efforts of his tormentors to dislodge him from his retreat were unavailing. They adhered to their policy of verbal silence, but resorted to every means they could think of except speech to attract his attention, to keep him reminded of their presence and to let him know that they were alert and determined. They pounded on the door; they showered handfuls of sand through a broken window; they put their noses to the cracks in the boarding, and sniffed with all the sound they could contrive to throw into that performance to let him know what it meant; they groaned, and otherwise imitated the sounds that are supposed to accompany extreme nausea. All to no purpose, so far as extorting any response or sign from him was concerned or provoking any movement on his part. What mental agonies he suffered, or in what smothered maledictions or silent tears his feelings found vent, himself only knew.

Finally, wearying of their apparently fruitless efforts to unearth their victim, they, one after another, retired to their games, their books, or their beds, and left Jack alone with his conscience and his humiliation.

Shortly after 10 o'clock, a crouching figure emerged cautiously from the boathouse, skirted the lawn in the shadow of the bushes, crept silently in at the back door of the house and, with bare feet and noiseless step, ascended to the "fo'cs'le aloft," as he called it, where Jack was wont to find rest for his body and oblivion for his perturbed soul in sleep.

When he appeared next morning, no allusion was made to the episode of the night before, it having been decided by the youngsters that the best way was to leave the medicine to work in silence. Before the day was over, they had occasion to employ their pantomime tactics in another way and for a different cause.

While Jack was launching the girls' boat from the float in the afternoon, he lost his footing and pitched headlong into the water. Fortunately, the tide was low, and he found bottom and got on his feet in water only waist deep. After clearing his mouth with a great splutter, and shaking himself like a Newfoundland dog, he broke out with a torrent of words that included the choicest of his vocabulary picked up on many seas and in many lands. Instantly, the children, smothering the merriment of his misfortune and the ludicrous appearance it provoked, and with faces contorted by expressions of forced solemnity and horror, simultaneously thrust their fingers into their ears and turned their backs upon him. Half-uttered words died away on his lips, and he became suddenly silent as if struck dumb. He climbed out on the float, and, pretending not to see, he busied himself about the boat in an aimless way shipping and unshipping the rudder, arranging the rowlocks, turning the cushions first right side up, then wrong side, sponging out the bottom, etc., and then doing it all over again, without a word.

"Is the boat ready, Jack?" called a cheerful voice from the pier.

"Yes, Miss," came humbly back, his eyes still intent on anything he could find to look at, away from the row of accusing angels ranged along the pier above him.

No one heard Jack swear any more that day.

From this time, there was a marked change for the better; and Jack's reformation may be said to have fairly set in. If he occasionally forgot himself, and permitted an interdicted expression to escape his lips, the quick thrust of fingers into all the young ears anywhere within hearing, silenced him in an instant and kept his tongue in check for periods of constantly increasing length, and, if he now and then returned from the village or the city with a suspicious odor floating about him, the sight of pinched noses, contracted brows and apparently nauseated stomachs sent the blood into his bronzed face to the roots of his hair, and awoke a vigorous mental "Aye, aye, Sir," in response to the voice of his galled conscience, saying, "B' the powers, John Corbett, don't ye ever drink another drop." The sign on his face was visible to all eyes; the inward colloquy, he revealed to me in confidence.

Chapter Fourteen ↝

"Have you ever had your picture taken, Jack?," asked one of the girls one morning.

"No, Miss, 'cept maybe 'twere a sort o' likeness pricked onto a shipmate's arm an' then 'twould pass as well for the ship's cook, barrin' the color o' the hide, or, for the matter o' that, for the cap'n his'self, savin' the rig."

"Well, Jack, how would you like to have your photograph taken, with all of us girls, with our boating suits on, and you in your uniform, and with the oars, and the boat hook, and the flags, and all the rest?"

"Whatever'll please you, Miss, will please old Jack," he answered, with more pleasure shining in his face than he considered it becoming to let his words express.

That afternoon, they visited the village photographer, with as many of the accessories of their waterside life as they could well transport or the limited area of the artist's quarters would admit of disposing to advantage in the grouping of a picture.

A great deal of time was spent in arranging the grouping to suit the combined tastes of half a dozen girls, an ancient mariner, and the artist. After much sitting down and jumping up again, posing in various attitudes, disposing of the accessories this way and that—all accompanied with infinite chatter—the group was finally arranged, to the great relief of the perplexed and, by this time, half distracted artist, as follows: The girls were formed in a pyramid with the eldest standing in the center draped with the stars and stripes, and the others kneeling on one knee, or sitting, or reclining, according to height, so as to taper themselves off gracefully on either side of her. The two next to her on each side held a pair of oars crossed over her head, while the two at the ends held aloft the boat's private signal and the signal of the N.Y. Yacht Club respectively. The youngest, and odd one, sat on the ground in front of them with the tiller ropes in her hands, as if steering the whole group, head on, into the spectator. Jack, in full man-of-war rig, towered above them, a little to the rear of the center, holding the boat hook on end, and looking like a gunner, rammer in hand, standing at quarters at gun drill in the good old muzzle-loading days.

The girls had given Jack frequent injunctions, on the way to the photographer's and during the arranging of the group, that he must keep perfectly still when the time came and not so much as wink an eye. This was a part of the performance about which Jack had many misgivings. But he braced up to it like a man, and did his best to make of himself a very rigid and con-strained-looking imitation of the sailor who poses on the left-hand side of the shield in the coat-of-arms of the City of New York. His lips were compressed with a look of determination and, at first, when the signal "all ready" was given, he shut his eyes tight, evidently thinking that he could keep from winking them better in that way, than in any other. The artist observed this as he was taking a final look through the camera, and with-drew his head from under his black cloth. He had a look of despair on his face, and a movement of his lips, which if it had been given voice, might have meant something emphatic. Jack was at last persuaded that the proper thing to do with his eyes when having a picture taken was to open them, which he did, fixing them in a stony stare that seemed to be looking into infi-nite space.

Then, as the critical moment approached, and the peculiar stillness that pervades a photograph gallery at such times fell on the group, and just as the operator closed his hand over the cap of the camera and began slowly to remove it, with the final, "Now, just as you are," one of the girls, fearing for Jack's steadiness, said in an admonitory undertone, "Now, Jack, keep perfectly still."

"I'm keepin' as still as ever I can, miss," he answered; and then, losing himself in the association of ideas which his erect and rigid posture, and the solemn hush, called up, he gravely saluted with a more than usual flourish of his right arm, at the very instant when the cap was quickly withdrawn and the plate exposed. The result was a rather pretty group of young girls, with something hovering over them that looked like an exaggerated centipede, endowed with human features and a beard, and with its surplus legs encircling its head like a halo.

This work of art is still extant in the family. Another, produced on the same occasion, in which Jack appears sitting cross-legged at the feet of the girls, with the halo attachment eliminated and presenting an excellent likeness of himself.

The summer wore away, and the time came when we were to leave the breezy shore of the bay for another home up the Hudson, but too far away from its waters for the continuance of the children's aquatic enjoyments or for their nautical appurtenances to be longer available even if the autumn chill in the air had not already begun to give notice that they must soon be laid aside. The boats were laid up; the fishing tackle stowed; and their lawn-tennis suits substituted for boating uniforms.

What should be done with Jack? He could hardly be laid up like the boats or packed away like the fishing tackle to await another season by the shore. Nor could he be converted into an umpire for tennis, croquet, and baseball.

The lady of the house attempted to solve the problem in the

easy way to which she was accustomed in dealing with the question of surplus attendants, by informing Jack that she was afraid we should have no use for him where we were going, but it did not work. She had been used to let her feminine assistants come and go as the exigencies of her housekeeping, and the changing seasons required, without a ripple on the placid surface of our domestic life, but she found it quite another thing with this loyal old shipmate. He felt that he had shipped for the voyage, be it longer or shorter, and it was contrary to all his notions of loyalty to desert the ship because the plan of the cruise was changed. He evidently did not intend that anything short of fetching up at final moorings should part us.

She gently hinted at reduced expenses.

"Lord, Mar'm, if that's it, don't ye mind a bit about th' wages. Just give old Jack a bunk anywhere, an' a bite betimes, an' he's yours to command. An' ye can drop his name off the ship's papers fur's wages is consarned any time it's low water in the pay chest or there's grumblin' at the reck'nin' at headquarters."

When she suggested that with no boats nor fishing there would be nothing for an able seaman to do in the line of his profession, he quietly remarked, "Maybe, now, yr'll have a cow to milk or a 'orse to be washed down an' to be given his rations, or a bit o' diggin' now an' agin, or a dab o' paintin' to be done, or brass work to polish. Sure, thar'll be something an old sailor, as is handy-like 'bout a'most anything, can do aboard th' new craft, to save ye a step here an' there, an' keep things trim an' shipshape."

She laughed "You couldn't milk a cow, Jack, nor take care of a horse, nor..."

"Look here, Miss—Mar'm I mean—beggin' yer pardon, I'm so used to be talkin' to the young Misses. Ye've never tried me at any o' them landlubber jobs, an' ye don't know all th' things an old sailor can turn his hand to when his heart's in it.

"An' there's th' cap'n, Mar'm. Sure he'd miss th' old shipmate as tuk care o' im, an' made things easy for 'im, when he was only a slip uv a lad aboard ship. An' the little uns, Mar'm—be ye thinkin' o' the little uns a bit? How be they to be gittin' along without Jack? an' - an' -" and here a choking sob and a burst of tears emphasized the pathos of his words—" 'twould break his old heart entirely to be parted from them."

The children, getting wind of what was going on, had gathered around by this time, and their pleadings reinforcing Jack's simple eloquence, the day was won, and to the satisfaction of all concerned. It was settled that where we went, Jack should go.

The mother herself was as happy as any of them over this conclusion, for there was a great soft place in her heart for Jack as she recalled the day when, with eyes streaming as now, he had laid in her arms an insensible, half-drowned, dripping girl whom he had snatched from death. She had really been talking against her own impulses in trying to persuade herself and him that we ought to part with him now.

In fact, the tender soil of Jack's simple nature had given deep root to affection for us all of which no one had guessed the strength. His generous soul would gladly have braved any hardship or peril—even death itself—for the "little uns." At the same time, Jack had, in his turn, burrowed into the affections of the family more deeply than any of them had realized, until the subject of his leaving us was broached, only as we have seen, to be summarily set aside by unanimous verdict. It now became apparent that Jack's fortunes and ours were to be inseparable while life should last, and no thought or suggestion to the contrary ever afterwards disturbed the serenity of his peaceful life among us.

Chapter Fifteen ✧

In the new life among the hills, we found Jack quite as useful and indispensable as he had been by the seashore. The variety of his accomplishments, and his fertility in resources for every emergency under these new conditions, surprised everyone. He came to occupy a sort of middle ground between the coachman, gardener and other servants, on the one hand, and the family, on the other, which is sometimes so important a field for the disinterested services of a loyal adherent in a large household. All the miscellaneous odds and ends of duties that seemed to belong to no one else in particular, Jack appropriated with an easy assumption of responsibility for the general welfare that was amusing as it was convenient. He awaited no orders and sought no permission for taking upon himself the doing of anything that he saw needed to be done, and took no credit to himself for it. The first intimation that he had thus assumed some new duty was derived from finding him quietly performing it quite as a matter of course.

He washed and swabbed the floors of the piazzas and halls—washing decks, he called it—sometimes several times a day. He would have holy-stoned them if he had been permitted. He set and furled the awnings to suit every change in the position of the sun or in the direction or force of the wind. He neatly braided and knotted the awning halyards in a highly artistic and ornamental manner, and trimmed all the floor rugs with fringes made from canvas, in the most approved man-of-war patterns.

The house was a massive-looking stone structure, modeled after some old French or German castle—a fancy of its original owner—with numerous round and square towers, and battlement cornices. On the highest of the round towers was a flagstaff, on which Jack made it a point to hoist the stars and stripes on every pleasant day. He was very punctilious as to the exact time for raising and lowering the flag. Every time he went to the village, he visited the watchmaker and compared his old silver watch with the correct time, and carefully set it right if it had gone astray by so much as a minute.

A few minutes before eight o'clock every morning, he would ascend to the top of the tower, and, bending on the flag, stand with halyards in one hand and watch in the other, and at precisely eight o'clock, give its folds to the breeze. Just before sundown in the afternoon he might be seen in the same place, with eyes fixed on the western horizon, and, as the sun's topmost rim sunk out of sight, the flag would be reverently lowered. He had a supreme contempt for the lubberly coachmen, gardeners or other servants on neighboring places, who hoisted or lowered the flag at unseemly times, or a few minutes too early or too late. He once suggested the mounting of a small cannon on our flag tower with which he could fire the morning color signal and the sunset gun. I had to explain to him that, formidable as the battlemented structure looked, it had not been built as a fortress, and that frequent gun-firing from the top of the tower might disintegrate the mortar, loosen the stones, and bring the whole thing down some day, flagstaff, gun, himself, and all, in a heap. He reluctantly gave up the idea. He came to be the trusted messenger for most of the errands to the village, as his memory was unfailing, and, without written order or memorandum, the commands given him were faithfully executed to the slightest detail without omission or error. He became

known to all the tradesmen, hackmen, post-office clerks, tele-
graph boys, etc., as the "Quartermaster of the Castle," a title
which he accepted with pride; and the proper authority for any
orders given by him was never doubted or called to question.

When winter came, with frost and snow and ice, Jack was the
first to be out in the morning after a snowstorm to open the
paths and clear the drives, to see that the water pipes and drains
were properly protected from freezing or that they were
promptly thawed out if taken by surprise in an untimely freeze,
and to see that the fires were burning bright and warm, and the
house comfortable.

Chapter Sixteen ✍

It was the fall of 1880. The presidential campaign was in full and enthusiastic swing. My own heart was in it to the full. In casting about for any stray votes I might influence, I thought of Jack.

"Have you ever voted, Jack?" I asked him one day.

"No, yer honor, 'cept it may be 'twere a matter of a round robin now an' agin, aboard ship, when th' salt junk were bad, or the cook put short rations o' merlasses in th' coffee, or th' grog was stopped."

"Are you a naturalized citizen?"

"Is it the right to vote ye mean?"

"Yes."

"Well, yer honor, I tuk out some papers once, an' then I've been told as sarvin' in the Navy along o' the war might have some'at to do with me bein' a voter; but I never rightly knowed as I could vote or not."

"What about your politics, Jack, Republican or Democrat?

"I couldn't rightly tell yer honor, which I be now. When I was a knockin' about the sailor boardin' houses down in the Fourth Ward, I was a Demercrat an' when I goes down there now to see Clementina an' gits along o' a lot o' my old shipmates, I sort o' feels that way inclined."

"What makes you feel inclined to be a Democrat, Jack? It seems to me that every man who fought in the war on our side, ought to be a Republican, as naturally as a duck takes to water."

"Well, you see, cap'n, its mostly all Demercrats they are down in Fourth Ward an' a bird's feathers is apt to be like them he flocks with, an' a sailor's colors is mostly them o' the fleet he sails in company of. An' then, them chaps as runs the votin' down there, us'd to come 'round the sailor boardin' houses a-huntin' fer sailors as they could git to vote, lawful or unlawful. They used t' say as how the Demercrats was fer 'free trade an' sailors rights,' an' that was what we wanted. They said as how General Jackson was a Demercrat, an' 'twere him as knocked out the British down to N'Orleans for tryin' to take all the Irishmen they could ketch in Yankee ships, an' pressin' 'em into the British Navy or hangin' 'em to the yardarm. They said as how the Republicans was all for the niggers, an' if they should win, the white sailors'd all be turned out o' the ships an' niggers put in the'r places, an' the'r wouldn't be no berths for us but as cooks an' waiters an' blackin' the niggers' boots. They said the Demercrats was for free ships, an' when we asked 'em what that meant, they said it meant as how the ships'd all be free to any as had a mind ter pick 'em up an' sail 'em, an the sailors'd be as good as the officers, an' have a chance at all the best o' the grub an' all the grog they wanted, an' they could sail anywhere to please the'rselves 'ithout botherin' about papers, an they could bring anything from anywheres without troublin' about duties, an' the'r wouldn't be no custom houses to interfere with 'em, an' the sailors an' the officers'd all share an' share alike in what the cargo'd fetch."

"And did you believe all that nonsense, Jack?" I asked.

"Well, yer honor, I can't rightly say as I tuk it all in, but the'r was a many uv 'em as did, an' that's why so many sailors is Demercrats."

Then I proceeded to make the best stump speech of which I was capable with Jack as sole auditor. I had no reason to complain of the interest and attention of my audience or of the result, as it accomplished what I imagine more elaborate addresses, before larger audiences, sometimes fail to do—it secured a vote.

"I reckon yer honor's right, an' ye can count on old Jack t' ship along o' them as ye sails with," was his comment.

I found on examining the papers that he carefully fished out of the bottom of his old sea chest, that only some slight formalities were necessary to perfect Jack's evolution into a full-feathered American citizen. These were carefully attended to within the next few days, and his hand was ready to cast as true and honest a ballot as any that would go to make up the nation's verdict on the approaching election day.

When the important day came, after depositing my own vote at the village polls, I accompanied Jack to the city, to pilot him through the reefs and breakers and treacherous currents that were likely to beset the course of an inexperienced and unwary voter around a polling place in the Fourth Ward where his wife's apartments, and, consequently, his legal domicile, were located.

I found that this was no joke. For three or four blocks before reaching the polling place, we were forced to elbow our way through noisy groups of zealous partisans, mostly of the typical Fourth Ward Tammany stripe. Innumerable packets of greasy ballots were thrust into Jack's hands, with vociferous exhortations to vote the regular true-blue Democratic ticket, and not to let the swell (meaning me) give him the wrong course. His dress and gait betraying his nautical character, frequent invitations to "Come in, shipmate, and have a drink," greeted his ears.

With a steadiness that under circumstances far less trying to one of his former taste for exhilarating beverages, would have done him credit when standing by his gun at the opening of a naval battle, Jack resisted all these blandishments, and followed close at my heels. As the fact that he was under my pilotage became more apparent, the jostling crowd began to suspect that he was really about to commit the crowning audacity of voting the Republican ticket in the Fourth Ward. Their attentions, already far more pressing than polite, were redoubled. Just how we got through what had become little less than a howling mob by the time we reached the door of the dingy hole in which the ballot boxes were presided over by an ugly looking lot of bosses and heelers, and got out again with whole skins, we were never quite able to recall; but somehow we did it, and I had the satisfaction of knowing that at least one Republican ballot had been cast in the Fourth Ward that day. How it was counted, if counted at all, heaven and the canvassers only knew.

Four months after the inauguration of President Garfield, Jack called me aside one day and in a confidential tone, asked, "How's he doin'?"

"How is who doing, Jack?" I asked.

"Don't ye know? I mean him as we sent to Washington to take command—him as you an' me voted for."

When I assured him that our man was doing himself credit and sailing the Ship of State in fine style, he remarked with a chuckle, wagging his head, while a gratified smile spread itself over his face. "I was sartin of it. We was right in sendin' 'im, 'stead o' the other one."

These confidential interviews were of frequent occurrence, and Jack received my continued assurances of the good conduct of the president with a self-satisfied air of proprietorship in him, and of a right to know whether he was doing his duty, that could hardly have been exceeded if he had owed his place to our two votes alone and depended on our joint approval for his continuance in it.

When the nation was thrilled with the startling intelligence that the president had been shot, Jack was wild with rage and excitement. He would not believe the story until I came home at night and he made me read to him every word of the reports contained in the newspapers. He wanted a special crew shipped to go down to Washington and try the assassin by drumhead court martial, and hang him at the yardarm the same day without waiting for judge or jury. And he made me promise that if this—the most natural thing in the world to his simple sailor mind—was done, I would use my influence to get him enlisted, despite his years. He even suggested that perhaps I could get him detailed as one of the gang to haul on the rope. In his then frame of mind, this he would have considered the highest honor that his outraged soul could covet.

"I'd sooner be one o' them as hauled on th' halyards to h'ist that murderin' cuss into etarnity an' drop his bloody soul into hell, than to be cap'n o' th' biggest ship in th' navy," he said with savage emphasis.

This was the first time in many months that Jack had been heard to use such strong language, and, as I then felt, I had little heart to reprove him.

During the President's brave fight for life against the assassin's bullet, in the weeks of sad waiting that followed, Jack used to wait for me as the carriage came up the drive and listen with eager interest for the news. The alternations of hope and dread which all felt in those terrible days of suspense found in no loyal soul throughout the land a deeper echo than in Jack's nor on any face a more vivid expression than on his,

When, at last, the long strain was over, and the wires quivered with the woeful words, "Garfield is dead," and even the bright sky of an August noon was like a pall over men's souls, I went home earlier than usual. Too sad to enter the house, I wandered out on the lawn. Here Jack met me and, bursting out with a vehement mingling of a curse and a sob, in his choking voice, exclaimed, "Yer honor, wot's this blatherin' stuff they be tryin' to fool us about down in the village? I don't b'lieve it—I won't b'lieve a bloody word uv it, 'cept ye tells me it's true."

"It's true, Jack. He's dead."

We were standing on the brow of the hill commanding a wide view of village, river, and mountain. Without another word, Jack looked away over the distant river, glistening in the rays of the afternoon sun. He looked over the hills beyond, their slopes mottled with patches of sunshine and shadow, and then up into the sky. He stood so for a minute; and then waving a grave salute, as if to some ascending spirit in the air, he turned away, and, with bowed head, and cap in hand, he entered the house, ascended to the tower and lowered the flag to half mast.

As I watched him from below, I saw him leaning for a few minutes over the parapet, and then, drawing the sleeve of his jacket across his eyes, he turned to descend. I met him in the hall as he came down the last flight of stairs. Without a word, he turned into the hall leading to the back of the house, and went slowly below to his forecastle in the basement, to be seen no more until the next day.

Jack was deeply moved by this event. Nothing within our experience or knowledge of him had so affected him. That the president whom he had helped to elect—the first public officer for whom he had ever voted and of whom he was justly proud—should be shot down in cold blood in the beginning of his career by a worthless crank, was to him, not merely a national calamity shared in common with fifty millions of other people, it was a personal affront to be personally resented, and he brooded over it as such to the end of his life.

Chapter Seventeen ❧

E arly in the following autumn, there was a wedding. One of the daughters—she whom Jack had rescued from a watery grave—was about to leave the family nest, the first of the feminine portion of the brood to take flight. This was the occasion of the next great sensation in Jack's life.

During the busy hum of preparation, he fussed and fidgeted about, much as a maternal duck might do when seeing her ducklings growing heedless of her protecting care and preparing to launch out on their own account. He hovered about the prospective bride at every opportunity, and betrayed the most anxious solicitude that everything should be "shipshape." It seemed impossible for him to divest himself of the idea that, in taking to the matrimonial sea, she somehow needed him as much as when boating or swimming in the waters of the bay nearly three years before.

When she was not down in the city shopping, his watchfulness over her was so constant and faithful—though so unobtrusive that she was hardly conscious of it—that when she was wanted for anything, and was not in sight, inquiry as to her whereabouts was instinctively made of Jack as a matter of course.

"Have you seen Miss Dora, Jack?" asked her mother one day.

"In the mizzen top, Mar'm," was the reply. This was his name for a little square tower at the rear of the house, in the top of which the young ladies had fitted up a sort of studio, the most scrupulous care of which was one of his self-imposed tasks.

At other times it was "Out on th' quarterdeck, Mar'm, with th' Leftenant." These were the titles which he had bestowed, respectively, on the front piazza and the prospective bridegroom. Again, it would be "She be down in th' galley, Miss, with th' cook," or "in th' main cabin, yer honor, seein' company."

When the wedding day came, and the company were assembled in the drawing room for the ceremony, some of the guests from a distance, who were not familiar with this feature of our domestic outfit, were surprised and puzzled at sight of a man-of-war's man in uniform, standing just inside the doorway, like a sentry on duty, intent on the proceedings with tearful eyes. Jack, in memory of the happy boating days, had rigged himself up in his man-of-war suit, as in his estimation the most appropriate way of doing honor to the present occasion.

When the greetings and the farewells under the mistletoe had been said, and the bride, after a brief disappearance, came downstairs in traveling costume, and made her way on the arm of her husband to the carriage awaiting them at the door, a solitary figure stood silent in the shadow of the porch. As her foot was on the carriage step, she hesitated a moment and looked back inquiringly over the waiting groups.

"Where is Jack?" she asked.

"Here I be, Miss, an' yours to command; an' th' Lord bless ye an' th' Leftenant," answered a voice, husky with emotion out of the shadow.

She stepped back, and, taking Jack's bronzed and tearful face between her daintily gloved hands, she raised herself on tiptoe and planted a hearty kiss on each cheek. Even the deep shadow in which he stood failed to conceal the deep blush of mingled embarrassment and pleasure that spread itself over his face from the fringe of shaggy whiskers encircling his throat and chin to the roots of his hair. The sound that accompanied this unaffected action was swallowed up in that of a great sob bursting from his breast that could contain it no longer.

As she took her seat in the carriage, he stepped to the open door and dropped into her lap a little packet, with one of his old time salutes, and a humble, "If I may be so bold, Miss." And they drove away.

As we afterwards found, the packet contained a pretty brooch of gold and enamel, in a curiously wrought device of anchors and oars and boathooks, with bits of golden rope twisted about them—Jack's wedding gift, and a memento of the old days by the shore.

Chapter Eighteen ॐ

During the winter that followed, Jack began to show signs of failing health. He bore up against it bravely, insisting that he was as well as ever, and continuing with his accustomed fidelity the performance of his duties, but the effort that it sometimes cost him could not easily be hid from the loving eyes that surrounded him. They saw with sorrowful intuition that something was amiss with him. His shoulders drooped, his step lost its elasticity, and the quickness that had once characterized his movements was gone.

He made no complaint, but, sometimes, when he was unconscious of observation, a deep sigh would betray the weakness he felt, but would not confess.

A severe cold, contracted while walking from the railroad station to the house on his return from the city one tempestuous night in January, had developed some latent trouble, or complication of troubles—traceable, probably, to the old irregular sailor life and its exposures, and, in some degree, perhaps, to a blow on his head from a falling block twenty years before—that baffled the doctors and defied their skill and their remedies. We saw him wasting away in a decline that we were powerless to arrest or check.

During this time, the patient and humble resignation, expressed in the softening of his rugged face, in the subdued tones of his voice, and in the quiet gentleness of his demeanor, touched all hearts. He seemed to realize what was coming, while resolutely

standing out against it with a sturdiness that was, yet, without
bravado or sign of rebelliousness. The old habit of facing death
with steadiness and without manifestation of fear, born of man-
of-war discipline and nursed in the din and smoke of battle,
asserted itself, and sustained him now in presenting a brave front
to an insidious and unseen foe, in a conflict far more trying to
human fortitude than the fiercest combat. He hardly ever spoke
of himself, and when allusion was made to his failing health by
others, he would listen in silence, or answer with a quiet "It's
nothin' Ma'am," or deftly change the subject by a reference to
some trifling duty that he had suddenly thought of as requiring
his attention. His face, however, betrayed at times, a serious
thoughtfulness that his tongue vainly sought to belie, and it was
not hard to surmise what occupied his mind at such times.

Once, and once only, he unbosomed himself to me. "Would
yer honor mind a bit o' talk, jest atween us two in the fo'c'sle?"
he asked me one night as I came out of the dining room into the
hall where he had evidently been lying in wait for me.

We went downstairs together to his room, where, surrounded
by his humble and characteristic belongings, it was easy for one
to imagine himself at sea, and to half expect to feel the rolling
of the ship and to hear the gurgle and splash of water on deck
overhead. We sat down on Jack's sea chest. We seemed more at
home together in this way, in the midst of these surroundings,
than if sitting on the two chairs that graced his room—more by
way of ornament than anything else, as they were seldom used.

"I've been wantin' to speak wi' ye a bit consarnin' some'at as
I can't help m'self thinkin' about, as things is gittin' to be wi'
this old hulk o' mine," he said pointing with his thumb in the
direction of his heart. "It be goin' to pieces yer honor, 'sure's you
an' me be settin' here, an' ther's no savin' aught out o' the
wreck, 'cept maybe 'twere wot I were wantin' to ask ye about.

"I make no doubt o' the'r bein' some'at o' me as is goin' to keep afloat an' drift somewheres, after the rest's gone down. I couldn't take no heart to speak o' the like o' this afore the others but you an' me has faced death together, an' thought o' wot might be th' other side, without tremblin'. Ye can onderstand wot's on my mind, an' never think as I'm goin' to be afeared now. But it's sort o' nat'ral as I should be takin' latitude an' longitude, an' lookin' at the chart to find wot sort o' shore I be breakin' up on, an' where the part o' me as keeps afloat is, maybe, goin' to fetch up.

"If it's a-goin' hard wi' me, I'll try ter think it be only my just desarts an' stand up to it like a man. But 'twould be a deal o' comfort to me if yer honor, as knows so much more consarnin' the Almighty an' his ways than an ignorant old sailor as couldn't never read the Good Book much to speak of, an' as couldn't make head or tail o' most o' the preachin' he's heard, an', he's bound to confess, never paid much heed to—if yer honor thinks the'r's a bit of a chance for me wi' HIM as they say died for sinners—jest how he come to do it, I never rightly knowed, but I've thought as maybe HIM dyin' that way might take me in—if I didn't onderstand about it no more'n a baby. I've confessed to the priest, an' he's put his hand on me an' said 'twer all right, with a lot out o' the prayer book about the saints an' the blessed Virgin. But I don't feel sartin in my mind as it's the priest an' the Pope o' Rome, an' the saints, or the blessed Virgin herself, as has the say about it in th' end, an' 'twould be a deal more comfortin' to me if, somehow, I had it from HIM if I might be that bold. I mind hearin' somewheres as when HE were a dyin', he spoke kind to a thief as was bein' hung alongside o' HIM, when he found out as the poor chap were sorry for all the thievin' he'd done.

"I've done a good bit o' swearin' an' drinkin' by way o' habit, as yer honor knows; but I never meant no harm along of it. I've thought may be if HE knowed that, an' if HE knowed I was sorry, if HE ever tuk it to heart as I done them things, an' if he knowed how I've tried to belay on 'em ever since it come to me as they went agin' HIS feelin's, HE wouldn't be hard on me."

We had, sometimes, since his health began to fail, talked over in the family his prospects for the future life, and had felt a serene confidence that the compassionate Lord in whom we believed would never deal hardly with that guileless soul, however imperfect his faith might be according to exact orthodox standards, or however his external life and habits had, in some respects, fallen short of lofty puritan ideals. I did not hesitate to impart this confidence to him now.

"HE does know all about it, Jack, and HE is not going to be hard on you, I am certain."

I took his hand in mine, and, in as simple language as I could, I repeated to him the story of redemption, and told him of the Divine compassion. Then I read to him from the Bible, the parables of the Prodigal Son and of the Pharisee and the Publican, and the story of the woman that was a sinner, who washed the feet of Jesus with her tears and wiped them with the hairs of her head, and the third chapter of the Gospel of John.

"Would ye mind readin' wot HE said to that ther' thief as was bein' hung?" he asked. "Not as I've ever tuk wot warn't mine, leastways not when I were in my right mind," he explained, as if fearing I might draw a wrong inference from his interest in that particular case, "but I were thinkin' as maybe HE wouldn't be no harder on me that HE were on that one."

I read to him the story of the thief on the cross, at the conclusion of which he nodded approvingly, and said, "That's it, yer honor; that's how I heerd it were."

He leaned back against the wall. His eyes closed, his chin dropped on his breast, one hand still clasped in mine and the other pressed over his heart. He remained so for a minute or two, and, when he raised his head there was a new light in his eyes, and an expression of settled peace and contentment soft-ened the rough lines of his face.

"It's all right, yer honor. HE's told me. I can't jes' say how 'tis in talk—I hain't much gift that way—but I feels it here," with a motion of the hand that lay over his heart, was all he said.

I did no more preaching to Jack after that. I felt there was no need. Perhaps, if I were to write in detail the interview above described, some disciples of a rigid orthodoxy would shake their heads and deplore what they might consider a sad lack of sound doctrinal teaching in my discourse with Jack.

If I had felt ever so much disposed to subject him to severe doctrinal tests (which I was not), he, in his vague, simple way, would have already forestalled and disarmed all that. He simply wanted to know how I thought he would fare with "HIM as died," and whether I thought God's compassion was wide enough to take him in, and I told him.

I am inclined to think that many a severer stickler for the dogmas than I am, or ever expect to be, would, sitting there with Jack in the gathering twilight, with that simple soul athirst for the Water of Life looking out of Jack's eyes into his, would have quietly slipped his Westminster Catechism into his pocket, and let the tender words, "Him that cometh unto me I will in no wise cast out" be among the first to spring to his lips. Under such circumstances, face to face with a hungry soul, it would probably be found true of most of us that our hearts are better than our creeds. God pity some of us if it were not so.

After this, Jack used, sometimes, in his moments of weakness or leisure, to ask the girls to read to him from the Bible. And when Clementina, who was a devout Catholic, or the good lit-tle priest from the village, visited him, he listened with equal reverence and attention to their reading of the prayers and offices of the church. This mixing of the religions did not seem to trouble Jack in the least, while we were glad to have him enjoy all the comfort and peace that both could give him, and were pleased to notice that Clementina and even the priest seemed to view it with like complacency.

But the end was drawing near. One stormy night in March, I was told on my arrival home that I had better go down and see Jack. He had been worse that day. His mind was wandering, and he was visibly sinking. His wife was with him, and, at her request, the good priest had been there and administered the last rites of the church for the dying.

I went down to his room. He was just then apparently in a quiet sleep. As I sat down by his bed, he opened his eyes and looked at me. He recognized me, but the recognition was of the old time, not of the present.

"I'm glad ye've come below, boy. It's a wild night on deck for the likes o' ye, an' it's better for ye here, 'cept all hands be called, then we must do our duty, blow high or blow low. Thar she pipes," as a fresh gust of wind shook the window frame and a storm of sleet beat against the glass. "The to'gall'n' s'ls was furled half an hour ago, an' the mains'l's jes' been clewed up an' the' watch on deck's aloft a-furlin' it. 'Twill be all hands on deck an' double reefs in tops'ls next—maybe loose reefs. Keep yer oil skins an' boots on, boy, an' be ready when we're called. If ye go on the tops'l yard tonight—an' ye're sartin to, ye'rs al'a's such a for'ard little chap—keep close ter me, an' don't ye mind grab-bin' onter me, if yer hold o' somethin' else gives way. I'll hold on for both of us.

"There she pipes agin, an Lord, how the sea's a gittin' up; that last one must 'a' swept her fore an' aft. Hark! That's the cap'n's voice a shoutin' now. It's lively times when he's on deck this time o' night.

"Hark agin boy, wot's that? Is it John Corbett they be callin', 'st'd o' all hands? It's the cap'n, sure's you an' me be settin' here." He raised himself in the bed, and listening for a moment with one hand to his ear, shouted with the old ring in his voice, "Aye, aye, Sir, I be comin," and fell back.

There was a quivering of the limbs a heaving of the chest, a gasp, and then stillness. I felt his pulse; it was motionless. I laid my hand over his heart. A faint flutter, hardly perceptible, met my touch for an instant, and was gone.

Jack's soul had gone ALOFT.

ILLUSTRATIONS

THE *NEW WORLD*

This original photograph of the Swallow Tail Line Packet *New World* in Liverpool belonged to Mrs. Dora E. Chamberlain, whose husband, Captain James H. Chamberlain, long served aboard the ship. Certainly this is one of the first photographs of a tall ship ever taken.

THE EMBARKATION, WATERLOO DOCK, LIVERPOOL
The passengers have undergone inspection, and many of them have
taken up their quarters on board for twenty-four hours previously.
—*Illustrated London News,* July 6, 1850. Reprinted with permission.

THE DEPARTURE FROM LIVERPOOL
As the ship is towed out, hats are raised, handkerchiefs are waved, and
a loud and long-continued shout of farewell is raised from the shore,
and cordially responded to from the ship.
—*Illustrated London News,* July 6, 1850. Reprinted with permission.

ALFREDERICK SMITH (A.S.) HATCH, (1829–1904).
Hatch married Theodosia Ruggles in 1854. Their various residences
included 49 Park Avenue in New York, a house in Newport, Rhode
Island, and the Castle in Tarrytown, New York, 1880–1888

DORA HATCH

RESOLUTE

A.S. Hatch's yacht, *Resolute*, 1871 (J.P. Newell) off Newport, Rhode Island

THE CASTLE, TARRYTOWN, NEW YORK.

Home of Alfrederick Smith Hatch, 1880–1888. Later sold to become Miss Mason's School for Girls, whose most illustrious student was Clare Booth Luce. It has since been demolished.

JANE HATCH, LOUISE HATCH
MARY HATCH, DORA HATCH
JACK CORBETT

THE HATCH FAMILY, 1870–71, Eastman Johnson (1824–1906)
From left to right: Will (looks like he is knitting); John (about to go out the door; he looks exactly like his distant cousin several times removed, Senator Orrin Hatch of Utah); Grandma Ruggles; Grandpa, Dr. Horace Hatch (who sent his asthmatic son to sea in 1849); Louise (Mrs. George Preston); Frederic; Theodosia (called Dora) holding Emily Nichols Hatch (baby); Alfrederick Smith Hatch; Theodosia Ruggles Hatch (elbow on mantle); Edward (standing in front of her with horn); Jessamine (with her hand on her mother's skirt; displaced from Dora's lap by baby Emily and repainted here); Mary (with magazine); Horace (on the floor); Jane.

HELPING HAND FOR MEN
MISSION HOUSE
The original building A. S. Hatch bought for Jerry McAuley at 13 Water Street in 1872, that became the first rescue mission in the United States and the model for hundreds of such organizations around the world.

HARVEY FISK, 1831–1890. A.S. Hatch's business partner for 23 years. (Courtesy New York Historical Society)

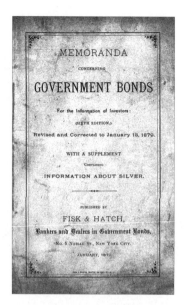

FISK & HATCH PUBLICATION *Published in 1879, a few months before Jack Corbett came back into the life of A.S. Hatch. (Courtesy New York Historical Society)*

THE HOWARD MISSION AND HOME FOR LITTLE WANDERERS
37 New Bowery, New York, New York. A.S. Hatch was president of the organization for years.

JERRY McAULEY, 1839–1884.
Founder of the Water Street Mission.

A. S. Hatch and Theodosia Ruggles Hatch in later years.

AFTERWORD
by Denny Hatch

The catalyst for Alfrederick Smith Hatch's voyage on the *New World* was very likely Richard Henry Dana, Jr. In 1833, Dana contracted measles and was unable to continue with his studies at Harvard College. He begins *Two Years Before the Mast:*

> *The fourteenth of August was the day fixed on for the sailing of the brig,* Pilgrim, *on her voyage from Boston round Cape Horn, to the western coast of North America. As she was to get underway early in the afternoon, I made my appearance on board at twelve o'clock, in full sea rig, with my chest, containing an outfit for a two or three years' voyage, which I had undertaken from a determination to cure, if possible, by an entire change of life, and by a long absence from books, with plenty of hard work, plain food, and open air, a weakness of the eyes, which had obliged me to give up my studies, and which no medical aid seemed likely to remedy.*

Dana's book was published to widespread acclaim in 1840 and was undoubtedly read by Horace Hatch, a prosperous and respected Vermont doctor. Nine years later Dr. Hatch determined that his asthmatic 20-year-old son should undertake a sea voyage that would "either cure him or kill him."

The *New World*
The *New World* was built in the Boston Shipyard of Donald McKay, who has been called the greatest naval architect and

master shipbuilder in the history of America. The *New World* was launched September 5, 1846. She was a three-masted, 1,407-ton monster, 187 feet in length with a 40-foot beam, and drew 28 feet of water. The *New World* was the first three-decked merchant ship ever built in an American shipyard and was the largest sailing vessel in the United States at that time. Before she was commissioned, the *New World* was sold to the owners of the Swallow Tail Line: Henry Grinnell, Joseph Minturn, and their partner (who had the unlikely name of Mr. Preserved Fish). Grinnell and Minturn were owners of the legendary clipper ship *Flying Cloud*, also built at the McKay shipyard.

In his master's thesis for Université Rennes, Landry Préteseille writes:

> *By 1850 the packets had become almost entirely emigrant ships, and new packets were particularly built for that trade. Though the word packet does not describe a type of ship, a type did evolve, and the packet and the clipper became the best known kinds of American vessel. There was nothing to stop an Atlantic packet being a clipper, but she rarely was. Both clipper and packet were full-rigged ships, that is to say vessels with three masts, square-rigged.*
>
> *By the early 1850s the clipper had much influenced the design of the packet, but no extreme clipper was ever successful in the packet service. Clippers were too sharp-built and too loftily sparred for the North Atlantic. They were built for speed, but their sharp bows, made to cleave through the water, were also apt to cleave under it. Clippers shipped water. They were wet vessels, and too easily strained by the buffeting of the North Atlantic.*
>
> *The packet became typically more rounded in the bow, and more buoyant and dry. The characteristic packet bow was apple-cheeked, with a convex bulge rather than the slender taper of the clipper. The packets were given stouter hulls, and more room for passengers and cargo. Their masts were lower than the clippers' and they carried*

less canvas. Their absolute speed was deliberately reduced by this design, but in fact, because they rode the Atlantic weather more easily, they were, over a voyage, faster than clippers on that route. The clipper attracted the legends and the painters of ships' portraits. The packets more often made a profit.

A. S. Hatch was lucky to have met up with Jack Corbett and gotten a berth on the *New World*. According to the *Illustrated London News* (July 6, 1850), a total of 219,450 emigrants left the United Kingdom for the United States in the year 1849. The majority of them were the desperately poor victims of the great Potato Famine, the wretched refuse of Ireland's teeming shores. It was during this period that steam-powered ships were gradually replacing sail and catering to well-to-do travelers, leaving the poor emigrants to go on the tall ships. Many of them wound up on "coffin ships": vessels that never made it because they were shoddily built and poorly commanded. In *Jack Corbett, Mariner* Hatch recounts how he narrowly missed shipping out on the *Brewster*, a ship that was never heard from again.

A. S. Hatch's extraordinary life following his adventures at sea

During early years of the Civil War, Hatch formed a partnership with Harvey Fisk (not to be confused with the notorious Robber Baron Jim Fisk). Working with Philadelphia financier Jay Cooke, the firm of Fisk & Hatch was a major fundraiser for the Union in the Civil War. Subsequently the firm turned the techniques perfected during the War Between the States to financing the transcontinental railroad.

Ten years prior to the reappearance of Jack Corbett in his life, Hatch, at age 42, was in his prime as family man, banker and big spender. The partners drew salaries of $33,000 each, which today would be the equivalent of approximately $660,000. Hatch kept meticulous financial records in a set of leather-bound ledgers with tiny brass locks, stamped with his name in gold. Every penny he spent over thirty years was accounted for. The four books are in the possession of his great-granddaughter, Jessamine (Susy) Brandt, and are truly fascinating documents. It turns out the salary was just the tip of the iceberg. For example, in 1865, he recorded income of salary, profits from Fisk & Hatch plus some small miscellaneous revenues totaling $127,312.80. With no income taxes, this was pure velvet: the equivalent of more than $5,000,000 gross today. In the income portion of the ledger for that year were entries for $75,000 and $50,000 and well as $1.00 interest from a loan to T. L. Snyder.

The Hatch family portrait

In 1870, A. S. Hatch commissioned the celebrated American artist Eastman Johnson to paint a group portrait of his family, including Dr. Horace Hatch, who had sent him to sea twenty-one years earlier. The fee was $10,000, or roughly $200,000 in today's dollars. When Emily was born, Johnson was recalled and paid an additional $1000 to rearrange the picture and include the new baby in her christening dress. The catalog of New York's Metropolitan Museum of Art, where the painting now hangs in the American Wing, describes the work as follows:

The Hatch Family, 1870–71
Eastman Johnson (1824–1906)
Oil on canvas; 36 x 50 1/4 in. (91.4 x 127.6 cm)
Gift of Frederic H. Hatch, 1926 (26.97)
Among the finest paintings in Alfrederick Hatch's art collection was this imposing group portrait, which shows three generations of

his family. It depicts them in the library of their New York resi-
dence at 49 Park Avenue on the northeast corner of 39th Street.
Hatch is seated to the right at his desk, and his wife, the former
Theodosia Ruggles (1829–1908), leans on the mantel. Her
mother is portrayed at her knitting and his father reads a paper in
front of the window. The most elaborate of Johnson's informal
group portraits in a domestic interior, the painting stems from the
tradition of eighteenth-century English conversation pieces and sev-
enteenth-century Dutch interiors. Johnson painted it with the high
finish and meticulous draftsmanship for which he was highly
renowned.

To see the portrait in color, visit the Metropolitan Museum of Art:
http://www.metmuseum.org/collections/view1.asp?dep=2&full=
0&item=26%2E97

The Yachts

In *Jack Corbett, Mariner* there are several mentions of A. S.
Hatch's yachts. In the ledgers, I was able to find records of four
yachts: *Escort* (1866–69), *Calypso* (1866–68), *Resolute*
(1871–73), and the sloop *Jack Shaw* (1872–77). Of the four,
Resolute was the most lavish and set Hatch back a total of
$53,306.91 (the equivalent of over $1,000,000 today) plus, of
course, running expenses that included salaries for captain and
crew, uniforms, endless repairs, and "sundries."

In an unpublished memoir, Hatch's grandson Alden writes:

Sailing was a great part of their lives. About 1866, Grandpa
acquired a schooner yacht that he christened Calypso *after Ulysses'*
sea nymph. As is the way of yachtsmen, Grandfather soon got a
bigger and better boat, the schooner Resolute, *108 feet long with*
a crew of twelve. Grandfather loved her like nothing before or since.

In 1870, he sailed Calypso *in the first America's Cup race in the United States, wherein the British yacht,* Cambria, *challenged for the America's cup. Because the America had defeated the entire Royal Yacht Club in a race around the Isle of Wight, the Englishman had to race the whole New York Yacht Club fleet in New York harbor. As Grandfather described the race, every American skipper but one thought only of blanketing the Britisher. The poor chap never had a chance. The little American sloop* Magic, *tending strictly to business, slipped through the fleet and won the race. The Britisher finished twelfth and Grandpa came in fifteenth.*

Temporary setback

The great Wall Street Panic of 1873 came along two years later and temporarily put Hatch & Fisk into what today would be called Chapter 11. From Alden Hatch's memoir:

The first failure of Fisk and Hatch shattered some of Grandfather's confidence and put something of a crimp in his operations. No longer did he spend money like Sailor Jack on a binge. Nor was he completely out of the woods. He sold the yacht and cut down his scale of living. The economy drive reached somewhat absurd proportions. In a household of that size even toilet paper was a considerable item. Greatgrandma Ruggles, who appears to have been in charge of retrenchment, decreed that no one could use more than one piece per sitting. This caused a revolt in the household; the older children demanded three pieces.

A. S. Hatch, humanitarian

For Alfrederick Smith Hatch, the two voyages before the mast on the *New World* were life-changing events. The constant danger, the frigid weather, the brutally physical work, the burials at sea, the endless struggles against the power of the North Atlantic: all had a profound effect on the future banker. But what moved him most were the people, the guileless sailors who could not keep away from drink nor stay out of trouble ashore, and the brutalized refugees, especially the women and children, the wretched refuse of Ireland's teeming shores. When young Hatch was sent to New York for his adventure, his father's only admonition was that he go to sea under a "temperance captain." As a result of seeing the evils of alcohol, Hatch never drank and raised a family of teetotalers. At the same time, Hatch came to love what he called "the roughest, dirtiest, swearingest, drinkingest men alive" and to believe in the value of every human life.

Throughout his business career, Hatch was a soft touch. His ledgers from 1863 to 1877 record more than seven hundred gifts ranging from a few dollars on up to thousands for charities and religious and educational institutions all over the United Sates. A sampling: Morning Star Sunday School, $1,000; Building Fund, Church of the Disciples, $5,000; Chicago Theological Seminary, $1,000. He was also a heavy contributor to the Palestine Exploration Society, the Congregational Society, and the Seamen's Association, which received a total of $13,500.

Hatch went far beyond David Brinkley's dictum that people should make as much money as they possibly can and give away as much of it as they can possibly afford. He lived in three worlds in addition to his passion for yachting: family, high finance, and New York's demimonde. While siring enough children to make up a football team, he was creating vast wealth in the rarefied world of investment banking and big business. At the same time Hatch was an inveterate prowler of the dance halls, saloons, slums, sailors' hangouts, rat pits, and bawdy-houses surrounding the docks on South Street, the Bowery and Water Street. Hatch's objectives in this milieu of New York's lowlife and underprivileged were to preach the Gospel and save souls. He wrote:

> *I have myself spoken from the steps of John Allen's dance-house to a crowd filling Water Street almost from Roosevelt to Dover, and been listened to with quiet respect, where a few months before it would have been considered as much as a man's life was worth to attempt to hold a religious service in the open air. We held prayer meetings in Kit Burns' rat-pit—a rough amphitheater in the rear of a bar-room—with the dogs growling and the rats squealing in their cages under the benches, while Kit's customers, thronging his bar-room, looked on in respectful silence, any tendency to the contrary being promptly suppressed by Kit himself.*

Enter Jerry McAuley

Jerry McAuley started out in life as a river thief but was caught and sent "up the river," sentenced to fifteen years in Sing Sing prison. While serving time, McAuley had a religious conversion. He was pardoned by the governor of New York halfway through his sentence and set free. McAuley and A. S. Hatch met at a prayer meeting in downtown New York and became friends. In 1872, McAuley, who had a serious drinking problem, had a vision of opening a mission to help homeless men and raised $450 to get it started. When he realized that McAuley was dead serious, Hatch bought a house at 13 Water Street that had been a notorious dance hall, and it was turned into the Helping Hand for Men, the very first rescue mission in the United States. During the first year of this useful work, 26,261 meals were furnished to hungry men, lodgings were given to 5,144, and a great deal of clothing was supplied. McAuley's Mission (as it was later called) became the model for hundreds of such organization across the country and around the world.

It was an off-the-wall combination—a felonious Irish drunk and the high-profile president of the New York Stock Exchange, an ardent apostle of temperance. Yet their work continues into the twenty-first century. As Jim VarnHagen, executive director of the New York City Rescue Mission, the direct descendant of Jerry McAuley's original Helping Hand for Men, wrote to me:

The rescue mission movement, as we know it today, hinges on the foresight and vision of your great-grandfather. The unlikely association, in human terms, of Mr. A. S. Hatch and the McAuleys resulted in an effective work soon to enter its 130th year.

About the manuscript

Jack Corbett, Mariner has been floating around the Hatch family for over a hundred years in various iterations. Hatch wrote it by hand in ink and in pencil on notepaper—some of it blue, some of it on the stationery of Lord & Taylor (where he had an office in his late years), and part of it on stationary of the Delavan Hotel, Albany, New York. It was owned by the son-in-law that married Dora, whom Jack called "th' Leftenant." I figure he worked on it over a twelve-year period, from about 1888 through 1900, regaling family and friends with the story as he progressed. In Chapter 1 he writes:

When I had reached this point in my narrative, and was reading over what I had written to my assembled family one evening, my youngest daughter (aged 18) broke in with, "It seems to me you are a long time getting to sea, Papa . . . "

His youngest daughter was Emily and her birth year of 1871 was precisely pinpointed in the Eastman Johnson portrait. Add 18 years and you have 1889.

Following "Bob's Story," Hatch writes:

I would like to tell the reader what became of him, if I could. I would give a good deal now, after nearly forty-five years, to know myself.

His first voyage on the *New World* was 1849. Forty-five years later would be 1894, when he was about two-fifths of the way through the book.

Over the years, many typed transcriptions have been made by family members who felt the work needed some embellishments and explanations. In the late 1970s, my wife Peggy spent the summer transcribing the book. She compared typed versions with the original manuscript. Where family members had tinkered with the prose, Peggy went to the original source and transcribed it until she had a copy as close to the original as possible. She then assembled illustrations and we sent the manuscript out to a number of book publishers, all of whom said they thought it was wonderful, "but not commercially feasible." (This was the period when Patrick O'Brian was allowed to go out of print for the same reason.)

In the summer of 2001, Peggy and I were invited to spend the weekend at a vast private club, a preserve of rich New Yorkers and Philadelphians, the Blooming Grove Hunting and Fishing Club. It was founded in 1871 and is currently made up of some 25,000 acres of glorious woodland in the northeast corner of Pennsylvania. Our hostess produced a recently completed, very lively history of the club by a Bermudan member, Ted Cart. It was a handsome green linen volume with matching slipcase. Peggy thumbed through it and came to the list of founders.

"Who is A. S. Hatch?" she asked.

"That's Alfrederick," I said.

He was listed as follows:

Jack Corbett, Mariner ᧭ 253

A. S. Hatch 1871–1873 (F)

The boldface indicated he was a founding member. The (F) meant that he had forfeited his membership as a result of the great Panic 1873. He was not alone; twenty-eight other members' names were followed by the telltale (F).

When we got home, I reread his manuscript; it was better than I remembered it.

At a recent Hatch family reunion held at the Mt. Kisco, New York, home of Jim and Twink Wood (Frances, great-grand-daughter of Jessamine, the fourth figure from the right in the Eastman Johnson portrait), cousin Harold Hatch picked up a copy of the manuscript and data-entered the entire book. Harold sent me a diskette of his work, but on printing out the first chapter, it was clear that this was not A. S. Hatch's original version. So I scanned in the manuscript that Peggy had produced and sent it out to our wonderful freelance editor, Helen Real, for light editing.

Over the years, the book has been known in the family as *Our Jack* or *Sailor Jack.* Cousin Harold titled it *Jack Corbett, Mariner.* This was the name and title given him by the Hatch girls on the formal document Jack signed with his X, in which he promised to swear off salty language and drink ("Except that I may have a pint of beer with Clementina on liberty days, and no more"). This is the title we went with.

The New York City Rescue Mission on 9/11

On September 11, 2001, the Mission's executive director Jim VarnHagen and his wife, Anita, were in their car at the entrance to the Holland Tunnel when two planes hit the World Trade Center. Everything was immediately shut down and traffic was rerouted back into New Jersey. VarnHagen raised the mission on his cell phone and said that it should print up handbills announcing that the mission was open for business and post them on buildings and lamp posts as near to the Trade Center as possible. Hundreds of men and women came, many without shoes, clothing ripped from their backs, and covered in white dust. What was remarkable about the event was the role reversal. Instead of the rich and powerful ministering to the homeless, it was the residents of the New York City Rescue Mission that printed up and posted the handbills, and, when the victims streamed in—many of them movers and shakers in the financial community—this group of humble, homeless men got them into hot showers, clothed them, fed them, prayed with them, and hugged them. "No one rejected prayer that day," said VarnHagen.

It is with enormous pleasure and pride that all royalties from this book, after out-of-pocket expenses, will be donated to the New York City Rescue Mission by the Hatch family in memory of A. S. Hatch.

www.jackcorbett.com

You are invited to visit the Web site for more about A. S. Hatch and 19th-century American history. Included:

- *The History of Fisk & Hatch,* by Harvey E. Fisk, the son of Hatch's partner of twenty-three years.
- Landry Préteseille's extraordinary thesis on the Irish Potato Famine and the 19th-century emigration to the United States.
- More excerpts from the unpublished memoir of Alden Hatch that include new anecdotal material about some of the most interesting figures of the nineteenth century: J. P. Morgan, Mary Todd Lincoln, the actor Joseph Jefferson, and the notorious gambler Richard Albert Canfield.
- A number of illustrations, not included in the book, related to the life and work of A. S. Hatch.

- A comprehensive series of links to other Web sites that deal with 19th-century business and maritime history, as well as nautical bookstores and museums around the world.
- And, of course, you will find a hotlink to the Web site of The New York City Rescue Mission, founded in 1872 by Jerry McAuley and A. S. Hatch.

Sources ๛

NOTE: When you visit *http://www.jackcorbett.com*, you can simply click on the links and be transported instantly to the various Web sites listed below.

Association of Gospel Rescue Missions. *The Life & Mission of Jerry McAuley, Founder of America's First Rescue Mission.* *http://www.agrm.org/mcauley.html#reclaim*

Bonner, Arthur. *Jerry McAuley and His Mission.* Loizeaux Brothers, 1967.

Central Pacific Railroad Photographic History Museum. *First Mortgage Bonds*, September 30, 1867 from Fisk & Hatch. *http://cprr.org/Museum/Bond_Adv_CPRR_1867.html*
———. *Railroad Bond Prospectus,* October 1, 1870, from Fisk & Hatch. *http://cprr.org/Museum/Ephemera/Bond%20Prospectus%201870%20BCC.html*

Christian Hall of Fame, The. *Jeremiah McAuley.* *http://www.cantonbaptist.org/halloffame/mcauley.htm*

Dreiser, Theodore. *The Financier.* *http://www.bookrags.com/books/tfncr/PART59.htm*

Gibson, Elizabeth. *The First Continental Railroad* (Part I). *http://www.suite101.com/article.cfm/old_west/27482*

Hatch, Alden. Unpublished memoir.

HickoksSports.com. *History of the America's Cup.* *http://www.hickoksports.com/history/americup.shtml*

Hollett, David. *Passage to the New World: Packet Ships and Irish Famine Emigrants, 1845–1851.* Great Britain: P. M. Heaton Publishing, 1995.

Illustrated London News. *The Tide of Emigration to the United States and to the British Colonies.* July 6, 1850. *http://vassun.vassar.edu/~sttaylor/FAMINE/ILN/Tide/Tide.html*
————. *The Depopulation of Ireland.* May 10, 1851. *http://vassun.vassar.edu/~sttaylor/FAMINE/ILN/Depopulation/Depopulatio n.html*

King, Dean, with John B. Hatendorf and J. Worth Estes. *A Sea of Words.* Owl Books/Henry Holt and Company, 1995.

Liberty Prison Ministries Tracts. *The History of a River Thief.* *http://members.core.com/~lpm8998/jerry_mc.htm*

Metropolitan Museum of Art. *The Hatch Family.* Portrait by Eastman Johnson. *http://www.metmuseum.org/collections/ view1.asp?dep=2&full=0&item=26%2E97*

Morning Chronicle. *Emigration Experience.* July 15, 1850. *http://www.swan.ac.uk/history/teaching/teaching%20resources/An %20Gorta%20Mor/emigrationexperience/liverpool.html*

Museum of American Financial History. *Northern Securities, 1860–1865.* *http://www.financialhistory.org/civilwar/1861-1865/north/securities.htm*

New York City Rescue Mission. *History.* *http://www.nycres-cue.org/history.htm*

Offord, R.M., LL.D. *Jerry McAuley: An Apostle to the Lost, Personal Recollections by A. S. Hatch, et al.* American Tract Society, 1907.

Préteseille, Landry. *The Irish Emigrant Trade to North America, 1845–1855.* Masters paper, 1999 (sous la direction de Richard Deutsch). *http://www.uhb.fr/Langues/Cei/lpret1.htm*, the Web site of Centre d'Etudes Irlandaises de l'Université Rennes 2, France. The paper is split up among the following URLs: *http://www.uhb.fr/Langues/Cei/lpret1.htm;*

http://www.uhb.fr/Langues/Cei/lpret2.htm;
http://www.uhb.fr/Langues/Cei/lpret3.htm;
http://www.uhb.fr/Langues/Cei/lpret4.htm;
http://www.uhb.fr/Langues/Cei/lpret5.htm The entire paper can
be found on the *www.jackcorbett.com* under the heading, *Irish
Emigrant Trade to North America*

Public Records Office of Northern Ireland (PRONI). *The
Promised Land. http://www.belfasttelegraph.co.uk/
emigration/menu.htm*

Quinnipiac College. The Irish Famine Collection. *http://invic-
tus.quinnipiac.edu/irish.html*

Richardson, Albert D. *Beyond the Mississippi.* Canadian
Pacific Railroad Photographic History Museum, 1867.
*http://cprr.org/Museum/Through_to_the_Pacific/Beyond_the_
Mississippi.html*

Ross, Donald Gunn III. *East Boston and the New World.
http://www.eraoftheclipperships.com/page5web.html*
————. *The Era of the Clipper Ships,* h*ttp://www.eraoftheclipper-
ships.com/*

Smith, Ron. *Liverpool Before 1900. http://home.clara.net/ron-
smith/liverpool/liv_19_1.htm*

Taylor, Steven. *Views of the Famine. http://vassun.vassar.edu/
~sttaylor/FAMINE/*

University of Wales, Swansea. *The Emigration Experience.
http://www.swan.ac.uk/history/teaching/teaching%20resources/An
%20Gorta%20Mor/emigrationexperience/liverpool.html*

Nautical Terms Used in Jack Corbett, Mariner ⌁

The grandest maritime dictionary I have come across is the companion volume to Patrick O'Brian's Aubrey-Maturin series, *A Sea of Words,* by Dean King with John B. Hattendorf and J. Worth Estes. Not only does it contain an exhaustive dictionary, but also it is filled with learned—and wonderfully readable— essays on all sorts of nautical subjects and people from British seafaring history of the eighteenth and early nineteenth centuries. Several of the entries that follow are from this masterpiece, so you can get a flavor of *A Sea of Words.* It is truly a delight for all who want to become conversant with tall ships' history and lore, as well as for trivia mavens.

The very best glossary of nautical terms that I have found on the Web is the following: *Yachting Dictionary of General information,* by Dixon Kemp. The Manual of Yacht and Boat Sailing and Architecture (11th and final edition, 1913); http://www.friend.ly.net/~dadadata/kemp/. The other great nautical dictionary on the internet is *The Big Glossary* at http://www.sailinglinks.com/bigglossary.htm

A.B.—Able seaman or able-bodied seaman.

ABEAM—At right angles to the keel of the boat, but not on the boat.

BACKSTAY—A wire support for the mast, usually running from the stern to the head of the mast. The stays that support the top-mast with a beam or stern wind. The topmast shrouds or rigging.

BECKET—A piece of rope used to confine or secure spars, ropes, or tackles. Generally an eye is at one end; sometimes an eye at either end; or a knot at one end and an eye at the other.

BELAY—To make fast a rope or fall of a tackle. In hauling upon a rope the signal to cease is usually, "Belay!" or "Belay there!" "Belay that!" or "Avast hauling! Belay!"

BELAYING PIN—The wooden or iron pins, around which ropes of the running rigging are coiled, also sometimes used as weapons. Normally kept in holes on a rail, called a fiferail or pinrail, around the mast. (*Sea of Words*)

BITTS—The strong straight posts of oak firmly attached in pairs onto the deck of the ship for securing cables, belaying lines, and other parts of the running rigging. The chief pair, the riding-bitts, are used for fastening the cable while the ship rides at anchor. (*Sea of Words*)

BLANKET—To sail close to another vessel to windward and steal her wind, causing her to lose forward motion.

BOATSWAIN—An officer who takes charge of a yacht's gear. It is his duty to superintend all work done upon the spars, rigging, or sails. He also takes charge of all spare gear and sails, and sees that everything on deck and above deck is neat, clear, and ship-shape. He must in every sense of the word be a thorough seaman, and must know how all work upon rigging and sails should be done. As he has constantly to handle the sails and rigging, he necessarily has a knowledge of their condition, and it is his duty to report all defects in the same.

BOOM—A free-swinging spar attached to the foot of the sail with forward end pivoting on the mast.

BOX THE COMPASS—To call over all the points of a compass in regular order. To understand the compass points and subdivisions.

BULWARK—A vertical extension above deck level designed to keep water out of and sailors in the boat.

BUNT—The middle part of a sail. To gather up the bunt is take hold of the middle part of a sail and gather it up.

CAPSTAN—Drum like part of the windlass used for winding in rope, cables, or chain connected to cargo or anchors. A mechanical contrivance for raising the anchor said to have been introduced in Queen Elizabeth's reign.

CATHEAD—Timber or iron projection from the bow of a vessel by which the anchor is hoisted up to the rail, after it has been weighed to the hawse pipe.

CHAFING GEAR—Tubing or cloth wrapping used to protect a line from chafing on a rough surface.

CLEAT—A fitting to which lines are made fast. The classic cleat to which lines are belayed is approximately anvil-shaped. Pieces of wood with one or more arms fastened to spars, &c., for belaying to, or to prevent ropes slipping, &c.

CLEW—For a triangular sail, the aftmost cornet. The lower corners of a square sail; in fore-and-aft sails only the lower after corner is called the clew.

CLEW LINES—Clew garnets. Ropes used for hauling up the clews of sails.

CLEW UP—To haul up a sail by the clew lines for furling, &c. Also used as a slang term for shut up or cease.

CLOSE-HAULED—With all the sheets trimmed flat aft, and every rope that helps extend the sails hauled taut. Hauled as close to the wind as the sails will admit without shaking their luffs. When a square-rigged ship is close-hauled she is about from five to six points off the wind. A fore-and-aft schooner, with everything nicely trimmed for racing, will lie within four and a half points of the wind; a cutter within four and a quarter points. This, of course, supposes the water to be smooth and the wind of what is known as "whole sail strength." In rough water a vessel cannot be sailed so close.

CLOSE REEFED—When the last reef is taken in, generally the fourth reef.

CORPOSANT/SAINT ELMO'S FIRE—A light that occurs when low-intensity atmospheric electricity induces an electrical discharge on the masts and yards of a shop. The light was observed with awe and looked upon by sailors variously as a good or bad omen. (*A Sea of Words*)

COURSES—The lower square sails of a ship.

CROSS-JACK—The cross-jack-yard is the lowest yard on the mizzen mast. Pronounced "cro'-jack."

CROSS TREES—act as a spreader to the topmast and masthead stays, the dolphin striker to the bobstay and the strut to the forward masthead or strut-stay.

DOG WATCHES—The divided watch between four and eight in the evening; thus the first dog watch is from four to six, and the second from six to eight.

FALL—The loose end of the rope of a tackle, the hauling part of a tackle; also applied generally to the tackle of the bobstay and the topmast backstays.

FALL OFF—To drop away from the wind; when a vessel is hove to she is said to fall off if her head falls to leeward, in opposition to coming to; also when a vessel yaws to windward of her course and then falls off to her course or to leeward of it. Not used in the sense of breaking off, which means when the wind comes more ahead and causes an alteration in the direction of a vessel's head to leeward of a course she had previously been sailing.

FORECASTLE (fo'c'sle)—Refers to that portion of the cabin which is farthest forward. In square-riggers often used as quarters for the crew. In the early days of sail a castle-like structure was built on the fore and aft ends of the hull and used as fighting platforms, with the midships area reserved for rigging and sails.

GAFF—a free-swinging spar attached to the top edge of a sail to which the head of a fore-and-aft sail is bent.

GASKETS—Pieces of rope, sometimes plaited, by which sails when furled are kept to the yards. The pieces of rope by which sails are secured when furled, such as the tyers of the mainsail, by which that sail, when rolled up on the boom, is secured.

GUNWALE—Most generally, the upper edge of the side of a boat. In small boats the timber, which fits over the timber heads, and is fastened to the top strake. (On wooden boats, a line of planking running from the bow to the stern along the hull.)

HALYARDS—Lines used to hoist or lower sails or flags and the wooden spars (boom and gaff) that hold the sails in place.

HANDSPIKE—A bar of wood, used as a lever.

HAWSE HOLES—Holes in the bow through which the cables pass.

HOLYSTONE—soft sandstone used by sailors for scouring the decks of ships, after which the deck was hosed down with salt-water, creating a smooth, blanched appearance. Small holystones were called prayer books and large ones Bibles. The provenance of the terminology is unknown; the theories range from the possibility that the stones were first taken from the broken monuments of St. Nicholas Church in Great Yarmouth to the fact that sailors often scrubbed the deck on hands and knees. (*A Sea of Words*)

HOVE-TO—The condition of a vessel with her head sails aback, so as to deprive her of way. Vessels hove-to on port tack should fill or get way on, if approached by a vessel on the starboard tack; but if the vessel on port tack can, by hailing or otherwise, make the other vessel understand the situation, the latter should give way; this is the custom of the sea, but there is no statutory regulations concerning the point.

JACK-TAR—Sailor.

JIB—A triangular foresail in front of the foremast.

JIB BOOM—The spar beyond the bowsprit in schooners upon which the outer jib is set.

LEECH—The aft edge of a triangular sail.

LEE—The side sheltered from the wind. The opposite side to that from which the wind blows.

LEEWARD—The direction away from the wind. Opposite of windward.

LUCIFER MATCH—A friction match having as active substances antimony sulfide and potassium chlorate. (*Merriam-Webster*)

LUFF—The forward edge of a triangular sail. In a mainsail the luff is that portion that is closest to the mast. To come nearer the wind. To "spring your luff" is to luff all the ship is capable of, without making her sails shake.

LUFF OF A SAIL—The weather edge of a sail.

MASTHEAD—The part of a mast above the hounds (the projections on a mast which support the lower cap, cross trees, and rigging).

MIZZEN—A fore and aft sail flown on the mizzenmast.

MIZZEN COURSE—See Courses.

MIZZENMAST—In a ship the after mast or vertical spar. So also in a yawl or ketch.

MIZZEN STAYSAIL—A sail set "flying" from a yawl's mizenmast head to an eye bolt on deck forward of the mizzenmast.

PACKET/PACKET-BOAT—A passenger boat plying at regular intervals between two ports for the conveyance of mail and goods; a mail boat. (*A Sea of Words*)

PAINTER—A rope spliced to a ring bolt in the bow of a boat to make fast by at wharves, steps, or other landing places. "To let go the painter" is figuratively to depart.

PARCEL THE RIGGING—To cover a rope with strips of canvas painted or otherwise. The canvas is wound round the rope and stitched or "served" with marline (a light twine which has been tarred).

Poop—The raised part of a vessel at her extreme after end. To be pooped is when running before the wind a sea breaks in over the stern.

Quadrant—An instrument for measuring the altitude of the sun.

Quarterdeck—The deck abaft the main mast reserved for the captain and his officers where the crew is not allowed unless duty calls them there.

Quid—Chewing tobacco.

Ratlines or Ratlins—The small lines which cross the shrouds horizontally, and form the rungs of a ladder.

Reef—To shorten sail by reefing. Also to shorten a spar, as to take a reef in the bowsprit.

Reef points—A horizontal line of light lines on a sail which may be tied loosely around the sail or in some cases to the boom, reducing the area of the sail during heavy winds.

Reeving—Form of reefing.

Right whale—Any of a family (Balaenidae) of baleen whales having very long baleen, a large head on a stocky body, a smooth throat, and short broad rounded flippers. (*Merriam-Webster Online*)

Rowlocks—The fittings on the gunwale to receive the tholes or crutches (pins fitted into the holes in rowlocks for oars to work in) for the oars. Also known as oarlocks.

Royal—The sail next above the topgallant sail.

Saint Elmo—A corruption of the name of Saint Erasmus, an Italian bishop who was martyred in 303 and became the patron saint of Mediterranean sailors. (*A Sea of Words*)

Serve—To cover a rope with marline (a light twine which has been tarred) called "service."

Sheave—The wheel within a block or in the sheave hole of a spar, over which ropes pass.

Sheet home—To strain or haul on a sheet until the foot of a sail is as straight or taut as it can be got. When the clew of a gaff topsail is hauled close out to the cheek block on the gaff. In practice, a gaff topsail sheet, however, is seldom sheeted home, as when once home no further strain could be brought on it; a few inches drift is therefore usually allowed. In square-rigged vessels a sail is said to be sheeted home when the after-clews are hauled close out to the sheet blocks or sheave holes in the yard. This no doubt is the origin of the term.

SHORTEN—To shorten sail, to take in sail.

SHROUDS—Lateral supports for the mast, usually of wire or metal rod.

SKYSAIL—A square sail set above the royals.

SLUSHING THE MAST—Covering the mast with a protective coating of leftover cooking grease.

SPENCER—A fore-and-aft sail set with gaffs in square-rigged ships, as trysails on the fore and main mast.

STARBOLINS—The men and "watches" who compose the starboard watch.

STRAKE—On wooden boats, a line of planking running from the bow to the stern along the hull.

STUDDING SAILS—Sails set outside the courses and topsails in square rigged ships; called by sailors "stu'n's'ls."

TAIL BLOCK—A block with a tail or piece of rope stropped to it for making fast the block instead of a hook.

THWART—A transverse structural member in the cockpit. In small boats, often used as a seat.

TOPGALLANT MAST—The mast next above the top mast in square-rigged ships.

TOPSAILS—There are various topsails; e.g., large and small jackyard topsails, jib-headed topsail, and jib topsail. In the early days of yachting a square topsail was carried as well, but spinnakers have superseded squaresails. Schooners carry as well main topmast staysails in various sizes.

TRYSAIL—A small sort of gaff sail or sharp headed sail set in heavy weather. The sail set on the fore and main mast of square rigged ships and brigs similar to the spanker on the mizzen. The origin of the term trysail was probably that in heavy weather it was the sail set to enable a vessel to "try," or to make some headway.

WINDWARD—Toward the direction from which the wind is coming.

YARD—A spar used to extend a sail.

YARDARM—The extremities of yards.

DENNY HATCH is a freelance copywriter, designer, and consultant in direct marketing and direct mail. He is the author of three business books and three published novels. He can be reached at www.jackcorbett.com.